Critical Thinking

Proven Strategies to Improve Decision Making Skills

(A Practical Guide to Solving Problems and Making the Right Decisions at Work)

Marvin Underhill

Published By **Oliver Leish**

Marvin Underhill

Critical Thinking: Proven Strategies to Improve Decision Making Skills (A Practical Guide to Solving Problems and Making the Right Decisions at Work)

ISBN   978-1-990373-73-2

Legal & Disclaimer

The information contained in this book is not designed to replace or take the place of any form of medicine or professional medical advice. The information in this book has been provided for educational & entertainment purposes only.

The information contained in this book has been compiled from sources deemed reliable, and it is accurate to the best of the Author's knowledge; however, the Author cannot guarantee its accuracy and validity and cannot be held liable for any errors or omissions. Changes are periodically made to this book. You must consult your doctor or get professional medical advice before using any of the suggested remedies, techniques, or information in this book.

Table Of Contents

Chapter 1: What is critical thinking?

"The unexamined existence isn't well really worth residing."

- Socrates

You have probable heard the term important thinking tossed spherical in college or at paintings. You ought to probable have heard of the values and benefits of crucial thinking but be thinking "Well what's it?!" Critical comes from Greek roots which means that stressful and necessities. Critical wondering isn't whatever more than putting stressful requirements for the manner we count on.

To positioned it honestly, appreciably is questioning in a scientific and unbiased fashion of wondering. Most of the time whether or not or no longer or no longer we are privy to it or not, we think in a biased or maybe downright prejudiced manner. This wondering style is poor, deceptive and dangerous. When we learn to strip away this bias and to count on greater in reality we're

1

capable of be able to make greater informed and useful choices as a give up result.

Be cautious of your thoughts, to your thoughts turn out to be your terms. Be cautious of your terms, in your phrases end up your actions. Be careful of your movements, in your moves turn out to be your conduct. Be cautious of your behavior, on your conduct come to be your person. Be cautious of your man or woman, for your individual will become your destiny.

- Chinese proverb

Learning to assume severely isn't always best a information for you to make our instructional papers higher and help us to shape sound arguments at paintings, it is a dependancy that could absolutely exchange your entire existence. Just as this proverb shows, the super of your wondering either straight away or now not without delay controls the exceptional of your complete lifestyles and in case you need to learn how to live a better existence then step one is to discover ways to take charge of the manner you observed.

When most human beings recognize this truth, that the brilliant in their lives is decided thru the high-quality in their thoughts, they decide to consist of effective wondering and the regulation of appeal. They decide that the superb manner to harness the transformative strength of their thinking is to say mantras and incantations simply so no mind however extremely good ones can run via their minds.

We aren't going to do this no matter the truth that.

What we are going to be doing is a wonderful deal extra practical and empowering. Rather than brainwashing ourselves with thoughts that might or might not be proper, we're going to hone our wondering right proper right into a tool to apprehend the area for what it's miles and make the exquisite choices we're able to primarily based on this statistics.

We are going to be analyzing the elements of our thinking a excellent manner as a way to take a step over again and understand wherein we are questioning accurately and wherein we're way off. Then we are going to be the usage of our powers of logic to peer what conclusions we're capable of draw from new and extra accurate information. And in the end, we are going to be deciding on from our conclusions the quality which we recall has the exceptional opportunity to decorate our lives or solve the hassle that we're going through and then enforcing that.

The prevent cease end result of mastering to grow to be a essential fact seeker is that you'll have advanced and internalized a skillset on the manner to assist you to brief and reliably arrive at the precise conclusions. Because you start to assume greater objectively, you'll additionally end up more open minded to new and higher solutions to any problems you'll be handling. You might be capable of resolve hard issues due to the truth now in desire to groping around inside the dark you can have a toolkit which you may use on any issue.

We normally will be predisposed to keep in mind important wondering most effective as beneficial in the educational setting but the reality is that it's miles useful in all areas of lifestyles to make proper alternatives and avoid falling into autopilot choice making primarily based totally on culturally frequently taking vicinity values that could land us in masses of warm water. When we use those essential questioning machine introspectively the quit stop result is a greater correct and deeper information of our very personal morals and ideals. It will lead us to a country in which we feel greater congruent and prefer we're performing inside the right manner.

Chapter 2: Why important thinking is life converting

We have already stated the severa myriad benefits of turning into a crucial logician inside the closing bankruptcy however there are such a lot of blessings to thinking critically that they deserve a chapter of their very private! Even despite the fact that analyzing to suppose greater critically and objectively is an extended journey, preserve the ones reasons to stay dedicated in mind and you may have the inducement to maintain jogging on this skills.

"The more you examine, the greater you earn"

-Warren Buffet (0.33 richest individual inside the global)

First, being a important thinker will reason lifelong studying. It seems like these days just about everybody seems to be speakme about how lifelong mastering is one of the maximum critical subjects that someone can do for themselves however maximum people aren't speakme approximately why that is the case.

The motive that lifelong mastering is the kind of buzzword proper now's that due to the fact the tempo of the sector alternatives up, fast and non-stop gaining knowledge of turns into an increasing number of crucial Think of the center some time, again then someone may additionally moreover need to take a look at a change and practice that alternate their whole existence without analyzing very many new techniques. (Let by myself a whole new exchange!) Times have been slower then.

Even inside the route of the economic revolution humans may additionally want to have a have a look at a craft and exercise that change most of their lives in the occasion that they decided on to. These days the tempo of technological boom coupled with the advent of the net is making many professions obsolete... and rapid! Need a journey agent? There is a internet site for that! Need a criminal team to encompass your commercial employer? Try Legalzoom.Com! You get the element. These days many professions are going to be positioned out of organization through large on line companies so the capability to have a look at continuously is going to be one of the primary subjects you may do to guard yourself on this ever changing panorama.

Think of important thinking as learning the way to have a look at. From now on you could ask questions and draw correct conclusions approximately relationships, cash, fitness, achievement, and so on... By using the tool of vital questioning you may have a compass on the way to will let you recognise if what you observed you apprehend is right. In this way you may be able to validate your very personal mind similar to a trainer or a mentor would possibly.

This in no way finishing development will cause you feeling a heck of hundreds greater satisfaction (and protection) than if you had without a doubt achieved what maximum certainly one of a type people do and attempted to save you studying the day you acquire out of university. If you need safety in this new international, don't actually earn worker of the month, broaden the dependancy of studying and growing so that irrespective of what takes location you will have a marketable capability.

The 2nd purpose to investigate vital wondering is that it will assist you're making more potent arguments. Rather than doing what maximum people do this is committing logical fallacies and making biased claims, you will be able to use your emotions and anecdotes to lower back up your theories however not because the principle component in your argument. This is a terrific difficulty because of the fact now your feelings will play a wholesome characteristic in the argument as a strengthening element in location of the extensive element.

Not most effective will your arguments be higher put together, an awful lot much less emotional, and more potent, but you will also be able to pick out apart the arguments of others. When different people make inaccurate assumptions, inferences, or conclusions, you will now be able to spot them and definitely provide an reason behind the error.

Third, it's going to assist you to be higher at the factor that makes us the maximum human; cooperation and teamwork. A large part of going for walks with exclusive people is the capability to clear up struggle, and to unite humans under one commonplace cause. The capabilities of important questioning are alternatively powerful in each of those regions.

Conflict desire turns into much less hard with critical wondering because of the truth maximum battle is the result of a lack of information or a confusion inside the communique. When you are armed with the gadget of crucial wondering you may be capable of correctly tease out and restate the arguments of the alternative individual and then stay calm at the same time as pointing out the way you note matters. Being able to stay calm and purpose and properly-spoken in some unspecified time in the future of struggle are 3 of the hardest subjects to domesticate but as success have to have it, all three of these attributes are reinforced with the resource of manner of the exercising of critical wondering.

As some distance as coordinating companies goes, having the potential to break down issues and notice them as it have to be will located you in a function in which you are the visionary of the agency. Because you are the most effective individual who has the capability to virtually see all of the statistics, you may be appeared to because the man or woman with the plan. As a follower, being able to workout critical thinking allows you to look the needs of the crew and if wished, to make concessions on the manner to make certain that the institution talents nicely.[ii]

Chapter 3: 6 techniques to apply essential wondering in day-to-day existence

There are 6 critical strategies a good way to will assist you to take the competencies you may learn within the relaxation of this e-book into your every day sports activities sports and relationships Aside from the chapters on the basics of critical wondering, this financial disaster is the most essential as it transforms the summary idea of critical wondering into a few thing actionable and real, some element that you may take with you and use in your every day lifestyles. This financial ruin may be beneficial to return again to after going through the rest of this ebook in order that you'll be able to comply with all that you study.

Before we communicate about the 6 techniques, you'll probably want to capture a pocket e book or some component it's far that you use to take notes. These strategies are imagined to be practiced and retaining a log of even as you exercising them and your reviews in jogging in the direction of with them will noticeably beautify your revel in with this ebook.

Strategy #1Use you're down time to exercise important wondering.

We all waste loads of time however whilst you're prepared in line, whilst you need to look at TV, even as you want to do unproductive stuff like that, you have got were given an opportunity to workout important wondering and reflection. When you are operating a mindless interest you hate or doing any of the previously noted sports activities you can use this time to think severely about your choices throughout the day or a particular trouble which you are going for walks on.

One particularly fantastic use of downtime is to suppose again to your interactions and key picks of the day. Thinking once more in your interactions you may wonder in which you have been clean and in which you were ambiguous. Thinking back on your key selections for the day you could use the alternative machine you are going to analyze in this book to decide whether or not or no longer you made the wonderful alternatives you can or if (because of lazy questioning) you can've made better selections.

Cultivating the dependancy of reflecting on the top notch of your wondering will help you to look the styles of precise and terrible wondering and could permit you to remedy any recurring issues you'll probable need to your thinking gadget.

Strategy #2 Practice one hassle each morning.

Making a addiction of thinking through a hassle that we are having every morning is a first rate way to begin to use crucial thinking on a more ordinary basis and notice more adjustments in our lives. Whenever is reachable for you, each over morning coffee, taking walks the dog, or for the duration of your move backward and forward to art work, you may exercising your thinking abilities.

Use the tools of essential questioning to interrupt the trouble down, apprehend what the elements of the problem are and how it suits into the more context of your life and values. Most of the time when we're running via a trouble we make the mistake of seeking to remedy the whole thing proper away and in isolation. What we research from critical questioning is that it's miles an entire lot extra effective to break the trouble down and additionally to observe it in the context of our lifestyles, what it manner for us, what a a fulfillment choice of this problem should look like to us (and suggest to us!)

This method of breaking troubles down into their factor additives jogs my memory of an vintage African proverb

"How do you consume an elephant? One chew at a time!"

In the identical way that we destroy down the method of solving issues in our lives one bite at a time, we are also going to use the same reasoning to the acquisition of the ability of important thinking. How are we able to take a look at this ability? One day at a time. Before transferring at once to the subsequent segment, recollect one time in the morning every day that you can exercising the knowledge of vital wondering all through. Pick a time now and then revel in free to transport without delay to the subsequent section.

Strategy #3 Practice one not unusual well-known of intellectuals in line with week.

Working at the highbrow standards (chapter 6) is one of the maximum difficult aspects to becoming a skilled philosopher. These precis necessities regularly present a huge assignment to us due to the reality they will be now not concrete guidelines or "the way to" statements. Because of this it's far vital to workout those requirements day in and day experience as a way to clearly assimilate them into our way of questioning. You will have a examine all about the ones standards afterward however for now it's far sufficient to comprehend that they may be positive developments that we want to cultivate in our questioning.

The notable manner to do this is to paintings on studying one of the highbrow standards regular with week. Focus on certainly searching at how each of the requirements plays itself out for your verbal exchange and to your each day existence. Look at how nicely you're using the same old of readability, equity, and so forth... Make satisfactory to ask your self how nicely you're doing and if the solution is some thing however impeccable ask yourself how you can do better.

Learning all of the necessities and turning into able to apprehend them on the drop of a hat is a large mission an awesome manner to take some months of workout. After mastering them despite the fact that, you'll be rewarded due to the truth after studying to encompass the ones attributes you could get an intuitive feeling for while someone else isn't doing the same and you may be able to help them to decorate the accuracy of what they'll be pronouncing the use of essential wondering.

Strategy #four Strengthen your intellectual person

There are intellectual man or woman trends which is probably accurate individual inclinations to assemble, just like the intellectual requirements are first rate conduct to assemble. These intellectual trends may be strengthened in the proper identical way as our understanding of the intellectual requirements and they'll be certainly sides of the equal coin. On the best hand you've got got the outdoor manifestation (the intellectual desired) and on the other you've got had been given who you have become (the highbrow trait.) we're able to take a look at greater about highbrow developments in economic disaster 8

Strategy #five Check in along aspect your heart

Notice each time you're feeling any unsightly feelings and begin to apply the critical questioning tools to check the idea reasons of this sense. Why is it that you're feeling unhappy, harassed, annoying, indignant, and lots of others.? Even although this approach may be unpleasant, the feelings (and mainly the horrible feelings) regularly function guideposts that will let you recognize in that you need to be taking walks on yourself.

In the terms of author Steven Pressfield:

"Like a magnetized needle floating on a surface of oil, Resistance will unfailingly aspect to right North - which means that calling or motion it maximum wants to forestall us from doing.

We can use this. We can use it as a compass. We can navigate with the useful resource of Resistance, letting it manual us to that calling or movement that we need to take a look at earlier than all others."

Learning the precise thoughts and interpretations of sports that ends in the feeling of those emotions will help you if you need to shift to feelings you may instead experience. Ultimately, through diving into our terrible emotions we make stronger ourselves and additionally our functionality to apply our critical questioning competencies. Plus, mastering the manner to experience better isn't always half of awful both!

Strategy #6 Watch out for organization assume

Groupthink is a term which modified into first utilized by the social psychologist Irving L. Janis that describes how, so that you can acquire agreement among a collection, individual participants disown their personal beliefs and adopt those of the organization as a substitute. We are maximum likely to apply this fashion of wondering whilst we are with a collection it sincerely is specially cohesive like a sports activities sports organization, a club, a group of authentic pals, and plenty of others.

So how do you observe groupthink?

Some of the symptoms of groupthink are: stereotyping, self-censorship, unquestioned beliefs, peer stress to comply, and rationalizing irrational ideals. The foremost gain of organisation count on is that performing as one unit is frequently useful to accomplish responsibilities short and efficaciously (because of a lack of friction among contributors)

Look for the subjects which you "Should do" the cultural values which are foisted on you and that would or might not be topics that you clearly believe. Critically searching at those gadgets and people "Shared" values will can help you find out in which you vary, and what you in reality recall. That is to mention to construct a extra correct definition of who you are and stay a extra actual lifestyles. [iii]

Although Group assume is a natural survival mechanism that allowed us to collect strong tribes, there are a few massive risks too. The unquestioned ideals often lead groupthink individuals to make horrible alternatives and now not to expect considerably approximately any of their moves (preserve in thoughts the Jonestown Massacre?) In addition to this, embracing corporation anticipate over your personal thoughts regularly damages self-esteem as nicely because of the fact it's far difficult to feel a enjoy of vanity while you're disowning elements of your self just to healthful in. When you start to uncouple your self from groupthink you're making a effective flow into that feels frightening at the begin but will lead you on a path of important questioning and self-discovery that would simply will will let you live a greater actual and happier life.

Chapter 4: Common crucial questioning errors

Critical thinking abilties are especially beneficial when it comes to speaking your elements absolutely and correctly. It permits you to interrupt down and understand complex situations and the take effective movement on the conclusions that your gain.

There is virtually one danger with analyzing a manner to expect extra critically, and this is which you might come to be annoying your buddies! We all knew a apprehend-it-all at faculty, the child who truly couldn't face up to letting the manner a good deal extra she or he knew approximately any given subject matter than you. If you made any logical mistake they might maintain to right naturedly pick out aside every aspect of your argument and leave you each higher informed and indignant.

I don't understand about you but once I research some factor new be it a ability or a reality, or a hobby, I have the tendency to carry it up in all of my conversations!

It doesn't keep in mind if the person that I am speaking to cares approximately what I am saying or if they could't stand taking note of it. I genuinely can't appear to help myself now and again! I am going for walks to beautify this trouble of my conversation however it's far an ongoing venture. If you are some thing like me on this manner, then this financial wreck is for you.

When we examine important wondering capabilities there can be a time and an area for them and a time and location wherein we will need to discover ways to preserve our mind to ourselves. Unless you want to come upon as a apprehend-it-all and a cynic, right here are a few accurate hints that will help you hold your friends.

Tipnumber one don't issue out logical fallacies.

One of the maximum thrilling subjects you can do together with your new placed important thinking competencies is point out whilst a person is creating a logical fallacy. Whether it is an appeal to opportunity or an advert hominem assault, pointing the ones out could make you experience smart and it can moreover fall apart the credibility of the man or woman on the receiving give up. The most effective trouble with this is that while you are in a communication with pals you definitely don't need to smash their credibility, you don't need to harm them and you in truth don't want to arouse resentment.

The amazing component to do at the identical time as you be aware logical fallacies is both to certainly permit them to slide with the useful resource of disregarded with the resource of everybody else or do what I name the "certain and…"

I do not forget taking an enhance comedy elegance as soon as and one of the strategies the instructor taught us to preserve the story going became what's known as "Yes and…" In this method you in no way disagree with the character in advance than you however you certainly agree and then hold to nation your very very very own factors.

You can do the precise same element at the same time as you pay interest a logical fallacy, in vicinity of draw attention to it, you may actually agree with courtesy with what became stated and then endorse a fallacy free way of expressing your concept. This can have the prevent give up end result that there may be a logically accurate argument at the desk however it's going to do it in this form of way that the alternative human beings inside the conversation will no longer experience attacked.

Tip #2 don't use critical questioning jargon

One a laugh factor to do while you research a new skillset is to throw across the jargon you have got got found and that is a few thing that I first did at the same time as studying to anticipate more significantly. "Can you please provide extra clarity on that point?" "Some of these premises are beside the point…" and so on…

Using terminology that maximum humans will no longer be acquainted with and not used to the use of may also stroke your ego but what it absolutely does is make exceptional human beings revel in silly. Making others experience silly is the number one way to lose pals and to be a person that no character desires to be spherical. Let's avoid this in any respect prices and in desire to doing this, permit's honestly phrase any mind in common vernacular.

There are endless advantages to training the skills of important thinking in every day lifestyles however one hassle to be weary of is which you don't use those abilties too often.

Don't get me wrong, there may be some gain to the usage of the ones equipment brazenly to your daily interactions however for the maximum factor you'll want to preserve your new superpower under wraps like Clark Kent.

The simplest time that I pick out to bust out the essential questioning lingo and the logical fallacy gadget to show a person incorrect is once they get adverse with me. If a person is making an attempt to get a leg up in a communication and trying to show to me that I am stupid for arguing with them, then the gloves come off. All the equipment are honest game and I try and ask probing questions, discover the mistakes of their judgement, and pick out out apart their credibility, and their argument.

This is a easy concept but hold it in mind, studying important thinking is exceedingly beneficial and could definitely enhance the splendid of your existence however it's miles first rate to move away it out of wonderful conversations. Remember that there may be a time and an area to specific your new crucial questioning competencies and locating out even as to acquire that is one of the foremost demanding situations you could face as an growing philosopher.

Chapter 5: 7 steps to vital thinking

In this monetary catastrophe we are going to test a completely simple 7 step method to interrupt down any problem that we're going through and create an movement plan so that you can face it. By the usage of this method we can be capable of act a long way greater intelligently and our motion plan can be dictated with the aid of a deep and logical information of the trouble in place of an off the cuff emotional reaction. Here are the 7 steps:

1.   Is this a problem over that you have control? If sure, suppose. If no, forget about approximately.

2.   Figure out exactly what information you can want to treatment the problem and flow into get it

three.   Analyze the records you have got accrued and expand inferences from it

four.   What are your options as a long way as motion is going in the quick, medium, and long time?

5.   Evaluate the options, what ones are appropriate and awful, what are the merits and demits of each of the only-of-a-kind techniques of thinking.

6.   Develop a approach to behave on the trouble. And then execute in this route of movement. A plan to wait remains a plan!

7.   When you act, degree the outcomes of your motion so that you can make sure that your plan is on foot and if it isn't, then modify it. Now allow's check an example of a trouble that I had and the thinking that I used to remedy the trouble.

Here is the gist of the problem, I turn out to be in need of housing for a few months and had to pick out right away amongst 3 alternatives. The first have come to be to move right into a large city with five other people in a small house. The second modified into to transport in with one friend in a smaller vicinity in a smaller town. The 1/3 preference have become to move proper into a circle of relatives friend's residence with him and his son.

In reaction to the primary query, that could be a trouble which I actually have manage of. I actually have no longer signed any legally binding paperwork of any kind however have all 3 options open to me.

The second hassle that I want to solve is what information I will want to consider for each of these 3 alternatives. The most essential statistics which I want to comprehend is: First, how a bargain might I like my roommates and what kind of they would love me. The 2d is price, how masses would each of the three locations price me to live in. The 0.33 query is how does the location and residing situation of these three locations in shape into my extra imaginative and prescient of my existence.

Before we flow on it is precious in order to recognise that my best existence within the meanwhile is to be a bachelor who is building his commercial corporation, dating casually, saving up cash, and running on constructing a public speakme presence to help the attention of my service primarily based completely commercial company. Because of this, the dimensions of the town and significant vicinity of my house topics, so does the capability to have privacy for dates and for art work.

Moving at once to the 1/3 step, studying the statistics accumulated.

The first residence must fee me 800$ in line with month, it is a fifteen minute bus experience from the coronary heart of a big metropolis, I would possibly have quite little privacy because of the roommates, and my dating with one of the men is apathetic at super and opposed at worst.

The 2d opportunity, transferring in with a pal in a small area in a barely smaller town ought to best fee me 500$ in keeping with month, the house is ready a forty five minute adventure to the equal maximum crucial town, I must have lots of privacy because of his work time table and the truth that he too is an entrepreneur, and he and I get alongside properly.

The 0.33 alternative might be 250$ according to month, be forty five minutes from the town, have some privacy however in no manner hours of the day, I enjoy the enterprise of the own family buddy (a mentor discern for me) and his son who has some comparable reviews as I do on key such things as lifestyles, love, cash, motive, and so forth...

So drawing conclusions, we're capable of see that the primary alternative offers me the most opportunity to do public speaking, and in all likelihood to satisfy ladies as properly however it is terrible within the truth that it's miles very pricy and has a lack of privacy in an effort to lead me to conflict building my commercial enterprise and with bringing dates domestic. Stressful relationships could moreover drain me of power and lead me to not having as masses pressure inside the direction of my key consequences.

The 2nd house is further from the movement for public speaking but thinking about that is a weekly pursuit, the pass back and forth is negligible. The rate is notably much less (which could in all likelihood aid in saving up cash) and further to this it has the privateness important to artwork on a organization and to hold dates domestic. The sacrifices being made are the excursion to the city and a few social lifestyles that consists of more roommates.

The 1/3 residence has the benefits of being a super place to shop up cash and to work on a industrial organisation but has the principle detriments of being a miles less than extraordinary vicinity to entertain dates and buddies, and moreover that it consists of a prolonged adventure for public talking engagements.

Using the 4th step of the way we are capable of observe the ones. My number one priority is constructing my enterprise, located through an energetic dating life followed with the resource of saving coins and then by using public speaking, then through my social existence. Because of the order of the hierarchy, Because of this we are able to see that the fine possibility for me is to transport right right into a own family pals area, This would possibly provide me the privateness to construct my current-day commercial enterprise, the reasonably-priced rent to allow me to keep numerous thousand dollars in the upcoming months, and sufficient privacy to have a first rate courting life. The worst difficulty of this preference is the period of experience for public speaking however that isn't a massive problem for me at this issue in my lifestyles.

The second satisfactory desire may be the ultimate one because it furthers my dreams of saving cash more but at the detriment of the greater critical dating life.

The worst of the three alternatives is the first one. This possibility damages my capability to paintings on my industrial employer similarly to my potential to shop cash. The maximum important blessings are social however the problem is this isn't my primary intention inside the meantime.

Moving directly to the subsequent step I had to outline my options.

Because of the way easy lessen this case is, my extremely good options are to transport closer to carrying out the vital workplace paintings and financial exchanges to move into this form of three houses. Because of ways I see that my alternatives I pick out out to execute on getting a small vicinity in the smaller city with my friend.

The next step is an movement plan to get that residence that I want. Because that is a own family pal I recognize that if I desired an area, he might likely allow me flow into in but I also don't need to position him in an uncomfortable function of getting to disclaim me if he desires extra non-public area and much less humans in his residence.

So my motion plan currently is to have each different circle of relatives pal breach the assignment with him to gauge his initial reaction and supply him a low stress surroundings to deny me shifting in with him if he wishes to.

Then if subjects seem great deliver up the difficulty of shifting in with him.'

During this verbal exchange, ask him if he is probably good enough with me moving in and propose my lease and obligations in the course of the house.

If that works, make sure things are ok together along with his son (it certainly is maximum probable) after which glide in and begin existence there.

Keeping the closing step in mind, as I am transferring via the method of speakme about the opportunity of residing with him the most vital aspect to preserve in mind is that I will want to be very attuned to his reactions to make certain that he says positive not out of obligation however out of a proper choice to stay collectively.

This is a particularly pared down example however having this framework is useful due to the reality having a framework on which to hold your mind approximately a nice trouble will make issues easier to treatment. Learning to embody this questioning style might also additionally take a few paintings (and it's going to take time to get simply right at the usage of it subconsciously) however it'll pay you again through the years.

This thinking technique may be utilized in all styles of situations, from courting picks to one-of-a-kind career paths, to purpose placing. Using this manner, you may be capable of efficiently describe the scenario accessible, what you would like to get out of them, and the moves that you may take. Then you'll be in a feature to assess the numerous alternatives and apprehend which might be wonderful.

This fashion of wondering is a huge departure from the way that we normally think about our problems. Normally there's no not unusual experience to the way that we assume, we right now consider what we need and the way we are capable of get it. We might brainstorm some specific thoughts to get what we want however then we are able to certainly right away pick out the quality which feels great to us intuitively.

Learning to embody this style of wondering will extremely alternate your lifestyles and if there has been no one-of-a-kind abilties that you located from this ebook, this would be the most effective that you need to remove from studying it.

The first way that this wondering device will decorate your life is by way of the use of assisting you to overlook the topics that you could't control. The first actual query asks if you have control of the final results of a state of affairs, if the solution isn't any, it recommends that you skip on and give up deliberating any manner to act at the situation.

As insane as it's miles, a lot of us virtually invest lots of time and effort in attempting to find to change subjects that we haven't any manipulate over and now way to trade. By accepting the subjects which can be out of doors of our manipulate we loose up our mental schools and our experience of proper and incorrect from having to address those issues.

The 2d fundamental gain that taking on this style of wondering also can have on your lifestyles is that excursion will flow into faster. When you discover ways to pick apart and honestly recognize the issues for your lifestyles then what takes place is that you re able to flow into in the course of your dreams quicker. You will apprehend what you want and a way to get it higher than ever in advance than and in vicinity of creating errors you can skip usually toward your motive.

The very last way wherein this thinking device will assist you enhance the excellent of your lifestyles is that you will be succesful to feel good about all of the choices which you have made up until that aspect. All too frequently we sense accountable, we enjoy as although we didn't act in the superb way we knew how. Even regardless of the truth that we recognize that we might no longer act in the direction of our personal self-interests deliberately, we get the sneaking suspicion that we need to've one higher. By embracing important thinking we are capable of do better because we are capable of be higher informed of the scenario handy and the capacity consequences of all the moves we ought to take.

In the terms of public speaker Les Brown "If we knew better, we might do higher"

Now that you understand higher, go out and do better!

Chapter 6: The intellectual necessities

There are quality attributes of first rate verbal exchange and well perception which may be universally regularly taking place due to the fact the premise of turning into an extremely good philosopher. These traits are observed in varying degrees within the whole lot this is said in verbal exchange and in written language. We are going to paintings to apprehend and domesticate these inclinations in ourselves and others in order that we turns into the form of thinkers who are capable of apprehend in which communique is succeeding and in which it's far breaking down.

The first of those highbrow requirements is clarity. Clarity is the feature of being able to recognize what's being said. Do we recognize what you mean and might you in reality outline and express your which means in numerous amazing techniques. Can severa outside observers agree on what is being stated or positioned forth?

If no longer everybody is plain at the which means of what's being stated then there can be a hassle with the clarity of what's being placed forth. In your very very own lifestyles what you can study is that during case you are not expressing sufficient readability then people will often ask you "What do you recommend via that??" or they'll ask you to mention some issue in a unique way with a view to make the which means that that clean to them.

But the query pops up, what do you do if a person who you're speakme with is not being smooth? What do you do when their which means is out of place on you or others? The solution is to invite questions. Rather than say a few thing like "I don't recognize your meaning, can you are saying that clearer?" what you will possibly do is ask what are referred to as clarifying questions. Some specific clarifying questions are

•   What do you recommend by means of way of that?

•   Tell me greater!

- Why do you suspect that?

- How did you decide that out?

- What are some examples of that?

- Are you pronouncing that (restate what they said right here)?

- Can you are pronouncing that every other manner?

By taking note of the characteristic of clarity in our communications we will restore the most demanding of communication problems, whilst terms are confused. Often instances the cause that a conversation will harm down and the awesome humans will no longer be able to acquire some form of consensus (or maybe seem like talking the equal language!) is that the basics of the verbal exchange had been now not sufficiently clean.

When a conversation is not easy and the primary mind are not obvious to absolutely everyone worried, there is no manner to have a conversation about what goes on. Imagine there was a fixed of people all searching at great pics whilst questioning that every one of them had the equal photo. When they attempted to talk approximately what they saw they'll have an now not possible time doing so. Learning to create clarity in what you and others are saying is the essential step in important thinking.

The 2d highbrow modern day is accuracy. Accuracy is the capability for the easy facts to be interpreted as proper or fake. Is it verifiable or real? If you assert the average American man is overweight you higher be able to decrease returned that up with some statistics! When we talk without accuracy we're able to each be basing our arguments on herbal conjecture otherwise we may be downright incorrect!

The zero.33 highbrow famous is precision, is what's being said measurable? When you are pronouncing that someone is overweight or that they've a noticed the use of document are you in a position to inform us how plenty they weigh or a summary of the injuries they have been worried in? Unless we may be precise in what we're announcing then our statistics has little importance. If our facts is plain and correct however no longer particular then we are capable of not be able to make knowledgeable selections.

For example, if we reap a be conscious from a relative that asserts that they've maximum cancers and the medical doctor has showed this then we would be involved however the lack of precision is an trouble. Because the be conscious doesn't component out wherein and the way critical the most cancers is. Our relative can be certainly wonderful with remedy or simplest have 1 month to live! Precision is crucial because of the fact the equal announcement can variety appreciably with the moderate changing of statistics.

The fourth intellectual significant is relevance, is what is being said essential and relevant to the verbal exchange in question? How what does is being placed forth wholesome into the more communique? You would be amazed on the quantity of times that inappropriate statistics can be tossed into an problem and the quantity of chaos it creates.

When we bring irrelevant statistics into an trouble then the stop result is that the important thing problems turn out to be clouded in confusion and we can't make sure what subjects anymore. Using the above example of a relative with most cancers a chum may probable attempt to offer us solace through the usage of telling us that his uncle has survived colon most cancers for years! This data might be comforting however it's miles inappropriate because of the reality we don't recognize what type of most cancers our relative has or maybe in the event that they did have the equal kind then one guy's enjoy has no weight on the overall possibilities of fulfillment and survival with any precise contamination.

The next highbrow elegant is intensity, is your answer honoring how complicated an hassle is? An example of a hassle with little intensity is that the "Just say no!" Campaign which meets all the above requirements however it is too shallow. It doesn't recollect the region of drugs as an initiation proper, the relevance of them in in-business enterprise outgroup dynamics, the consequences vs rewards of numerous pills, and so on...

I consider a communication I modified into currently having on a messaging board approximately the problems surrounding wealth. The individual that I became arguing towards positioned forth the commonplace but woefully inadequate concept that the solution to the hassle of wealth inequity end up really to take all the money from the billionaires and redistribute it to the poorest people inside the global.

This solution must technically take care of some of the inequity but it does not take into account the stability of energy that unique international locations have. It doesn't recall the disparity in schooling and industrial enterprise possibilities that the arena has. Although technically actual, this person's argument lacks intensity and as such wants to be elaborated on and challenged on some of the more subtle elements.

Rarely are troubles one dimensional or maybe particularly easy, a protracted manner greater often they may be pretty complicated and require a remarkable deal of depth. When running to weed out overly simplistic questioning maintain a watch constant out for smooth solutions to large problems. They are nearly usually missing something.

Next is breadth, do you study the concept from numerous standpoints and factors of view? Or is that this a myopically targeted argument that most effective takes one mindset into account? We all understand folks that are too set of their strategies to recollect any outside information or views. This may be unfavourable in case your goal is to discover the truth and to apprehend a topic properly Having breadth to your thinking is all approximately taking opposing points of view and gaining knowledge of to entertain them as properly.

When you entertain opposing factors of view you'll get a greater properly-rounded knowledge of the troubles which you think about and be able to talk greater intelligently about them. You may find out that you have had a exchange of heart, and if you haven't, you may discover a modern-day manner to argue for your preliminary opinion

The subsequent intellectual full-size is common sense, does this sincerely make enjoy? Are logical fallacies being used? Does the notion continuously observe from the premises? Sometimes horrible commonplace enjoy is straightforward to identify but from time to time it is highly difficult to see! Sometimes an issue will seem real however the right judgment inside the middle is probably faulty someplace, or even one slip inside the commonplace sense of a problem can lead from actual premises to faux or ambiguous conclusions.

Learning to identify logical fallacies that motive wrong conclusions is a real task and it'd no longer be sincere to address them on this economic break. Because of this I absolutely have committed the entire next monetary disaster to logical fallacies, what they are and a manner to spot them.

Fairness, do I virtually have a bias or an hobby this is fundamental me to an unfair evaluation of this trouble? This is a problem which can be very essential and one of the toughest matters to accomplish in important questioning. All mind and all mind are visible thru the lens we've got were given got of the sector. Our perception structures change the way we see the arena and human beings encouraged the same facts might see it in fact opposing strategies.

It is of crucial significance to discover ways to see things in as easy and as honest a way as viable due to the fact best while we see subjects from a sincere point of view can we sincerely start to recollect our wondering. The greater biased our thinking, the extra extreme it is going to be and the lots less useful it's miles going to be for making cause critiques of issues and finding solutions.

By making use of those requirements we are able to understand at the same time as our questioning is right and at the same time as it's miles useless, while we need to consider our thoughts and even as we need to art work a piece greater difficult to make sure that we are absolutely doing a wonderful technique of representing the thing that we're considering and also of developing with conclusions from this.

If we don't feature with highbrow necessities when making important choices then we'd find ourselves going thru a alternatively dismal scenario when our emotions have led us to make a stupid choice that aren't quality for us or others. [iv]

Spotting logical fallacies when arguing

The strawman- Rather than argue in opposition to a person's argument what you do is misread what they say in a few key way and then you definitely attack this erroneous argument. This gives the illusion of you beating their argument while in fact all you have got were given completed is make up an trouble and beat it. An example of this is probably character A "We want to reform marijuana legal guidelines" person B "If we do that all the youngsters will smoke weed, lose motivation, and the whole society will collapse" Person B has taken a vague argument and misinterpreted it as "We need to take away ALL law around marijuana criminal guidelines" while in fact what might have been proposed is "We need to deal with marijuana exactly like alcohol" This fallacy is one reason why we want to make sure that we are precise and easy.

False Cause- I learned this concept underneath the choice "Correlation does not identical causation!" What this suggests is that if matters take place together regularly you faux like one reasons the opportunity. This could in all likelihood or might not be the case. For example we might word that every one mayors in our town have had mustaches and due to that count on that a mustache lets you get elected... In truth this is probably coincidence or the those who are associated sufficient to end up mayor all percentage this style however in fact it has now not some thing to do with motive

The enchantment to emotion- This is even as robust emotions are elicited to try to get humans to move in opposition to their common revel in. One example of this from my personal existence is that of the abortion debate. Regardless of your views, this situation is instructive. I changed into talking to a prolife campaigner and they stated "My mom almost had me aborted because of the fact I changed into the crafted from rape, are you announcing which you could have supported my being aborted??" This appeal to emotion have become designed to change my thoughts a protracted manner from a prochoice stance. Luckily I truely said "yes "and walked away.

The slippery slope – in this fallacy you argue that one movement will bring about a whole chain of various actions that in the end is undesirable. Because of this you argue that the number one motion should be prevented from taking place. A tremendous example of this is the "marijuana is a gateway drug" argument. Sure maximum heroin addicts have smoked pot first but in addition they have eaten broccoli. So because of this broccoli need to be the final gateway drug.

The ad Homonym attack- This particular fallacy is not unusual in politics. In this fallacy what you do is assault the possibility person's individual in an try and make people not be given as genuine with them. A commonplace instance might be in a playground whilst a infant makes a cogent argument and the bully says "Yeah however tommy is a bed wetter!" after which all of a sudden no quantity of common experience is useful in convincing the playground. This childish instance isn't all that some distance off from the attacks you could see round election season!

Tu Quoque- This is the act of meeting a complaint with a grievance. It avoids answering the accusations pressed in the direction of you and as a substitute attempts to divert them again at the accuser. An instance might be amongst sisters on the dinner desk. Sister A rats her sibling out by way of saying "Sally borrowed the auto without asking!" and then at the same time as the mother and father glare at sally she says "yeah however Trisha stole five$ from your handbag mom!" and by the use of a tuquoque fallacy may additionally simply break out with borrowing the automobile with out asking

The loaded query – Most people are fairly acquainted with this form of logical fallacy. In this you ask a question that could't be answered with out performing to be accountable. This fallacy rings a bell in my memory of thee shaggy canine story approximately an innocent husband who is being puzzled at a police station after being arrested. "So, whilst did you prevent beating your partner sir?" his alternatives are 1. I never stopped! Or 2. Oh approximately a three hundred and sixty five days inside the beyond!

The burden of evidence – In this fallacy you assert that the burden is not to show a sure claim is right however to try to make someone else prove that it's miles fake. A common example might be among Christians and atheists. A Christian could probably say that "absence of evidence isn't evidence of absence" and faux like which means that god have to exist. They ask the atheist to reveal that god doesn't exist and while the atheist can't control this now not possible project the Christian could likely count on that consequently god should exist

The bandwagon fallacy aka the attraction to popularity – In this fallacy you're saying that because of the reality precise humans had been doing a little issue it have to be the proper detail to do. An instance of this fallacy on foot rampant is that of the bloodletting which have become so well-known in remedy a century within the beyond. It began out off as a small fad and then as extra human beings did it the truth that such a variety of human beings were doing it emerge as proof enough for more to include the remedy-all

The next fallacy is the enchantment to authority – In this one you're basically announcing that because of the fact someone who represents authority (a medical doctor, an writer, a scientist, a pastor...) says something that it need to be actual. An example that I heard from a pal of mine presently become at the same time as my pal knowledgeable me that her medical doctor stated that doing crunches is horrible to your again.

The black and white fallacy- in this one you present options and make a person pick out amongst them when in fact there might be infinite sun shades of grey to select out from! I actually used this fallacy when describing the loaded question, did you notice that?

Begging the question – this fallacy is likewise called round reasoning and irrespective of how longwinded the argument the principle idea is which you are saying a few component is real due to the fact it is proper. One instance of that is individuals who trust the bible word for phrase (not to pick on your faith as a super way to stay life) When you take a look at most of these arguments they appear like this. "The bible is real and truly perfect. The cause we recognize is due to the fact in the bible it says that the bible is the phrase of god and due to the truth god is ideal, so is his ebook."

This is a ridiculous argument and even as it's miles utilized in exclusive areas it's far greater with out issue observed. This quantities to me saying that I am infallible due to the reality I said so and an infallible person can't say something that isn't proper. Absurd.

Appeal to nature – on this fallacy you assert that because a few thing got here from nature it have to be suitable. This conjures the photograph of a stoner saying "It grows out of the earth guy, it's healthy!" But one receives the sensation if the same person were bit with the useful resource of an all-herbal rattlesnake they may realize that nature isn't intrinsically appropriate or terrible for us.

Anecdotal- This form of fallacy is specially persuasive and convincing however moreover absolutely baseless. In it you basically say that because of the reality a certain concept worked for one individual it will art work for others. Common instance, my grandpa ate 3 huge macs a day and lived glad and wholesome to ninety nine years vintage. This doesn't preserve in thoughts all the distinctive people who won't have fared so well!

The affirmation bias- This fallacy is even as you start out with a premise that some element is real and then you definately virtually best pick data that furthers this idea in desire to all the to be had statistics. For example: Eating best bananas permits you shed pounds fast! You may match out and discover research that propose this and private recollections for delivered emotional and anecdotal appeal however while you find out a look at showing a thousand human beings won weight on the equal diet regime you quietly burn it and never communicate about all of it yet again. Confirmation bias!

Awesome highbrow inclinations to assemble

Just like we labored to boom our understanding of the educational requirements, we additionally want to increase our capability to embody what it way to be an clever truth seeker. By turning into the form of person who truely demonstrates the ones virtues you turns into extra likable, and higher at expressing your self. The belongings you say will glaringly have a propensity to return from a grounded and correct location and you may do away with the horrible highbrow behavior that might had been maintaining you decrease back from speakme efficiently in professional situations.

One idea that self-development massive Anthony Robbins describes is the importance of "Identity Level Change." What this suggests isn't virtually converting what we do or what we recognize, however how we view ourselves. The relaxation of the techniques on this e-book are important however this financial disaster is the best with a view to allow you to make the most important shift to your lifestyles. By turning into someone who clearly expresses these developments, the relaxation of the important wondering system will no longer be a few thing you will need to do. It may be an outgrowth of who you are.

The dispositions:

The first trait is Intellectual Humility We all apprehend what it is to be humble in our every day lifestyles however at the same time as taken into the area of purpose humility includes acknowledging your limits. Admitting which you don't recognize everything. There are numerous errors that even the outstanding thinkers make, we have blind spots to quantities of evidence that specific human beings can see without issue, we've got were given biases that skew the manner we see the world, and we've got had been given reviews that tint the way all records is interpreted.

No rely how tough we try, we can in no way be ideal and ideal thinkers and acknowledging that is very critical because it will will let you face up to the 2 poles of communicating, Being a susceptible communicator who doubts all their very very own evaluations and being an intellectually pompous ass. The former can't persuade every body of some thing and the latter may probable persuade but arouse resentment all along the manner.

The second key trait is highbrow bravery. It is easy to look at ordinary troubles under the lens of the critical thinking microscope but to examine thoughts or activities which have a strong terrible emotion related takes a high quality form of character. Looking at those troubles and popping out the alternative element with a clear head is like stepping into an unusual wooded area filled with wild animals, bandits, witches, and staying calm and gift as you pass all of the traumatic situations along the way.

Looking at the ones troubles also can be difficult because of the fact often the maximum hard matters to observe are the ones which is probably the most extensively familiar with the aid of society. It takes braveness to consider the values of society and observe if you certainly be given as true with them. Questioning the tribe elicits a robust reaction in us because it is one of the most historic and primal fears to be kicked out inside the cold by means of our tribe. We talked about this in the financial ruin about groupthink

One manner wherein you may find out and show the capabilities of highbrow bravery is to have a take a look at what the writer Steven Pressfield calls resistance. This resistance is the sensation of no longer looking to do a little element. Maybe we realize we must hit the health club or write our paper however we simply don't want to! Pressfield makes the declare that "Resistance unfailingly points to genuine north." This method that the trouble that we least need to do is often the issue that we need to do the maximum. In the vicinity of crucial thinking what this indicates is that the problems that you clearly don't want to reflect onconsideration on are the ones which will be the most valuable as a way to reflect onconsideration on.

The zero.33 highbrow trait that we need to try to cultivate is highbrow integrity. Intellectual integrity is the stress to preserve ourselves to excessive requirements. Play the satan's recommend, try and punch holes in your very very own arguments and display yourself wrong. Imagine that you are tasked with the hobby of arguing in competition to your self, how should you do it? Intellectual integrity is keeping yourself to the same immoderate requirements that you maintain your antagonists to. By embracing this concept you turns into a more potent fact seeker. This idea is similar to the idea of Kaizen in Japan, the precept of steady and in no manner-completing improvement.

The fourth highbrow trait is to boom highbrow compassion. In Dale Carnegies communication traditional "How to win friends and have an effect on humans" He describes how one of the most vital dispositions we are able to growth while speakme with others is to emerge as really interested by them. In a similar manner, even as we're jogging on building this person trait we're capable of want to in fact positioned ourselves of their footwear.

When we talk with others it's miles often times a tendency to push aside their factors and their feelings, specifically if it is a heated verbal exchange. We must fight this urge and instead artwork to understand them, and truely sense what they are feeling. Even if we are just reading a paper or a records story that has a fantastic opinion than we do, constructing the exercise of empathy will help us to make better arguments and moreover to adopt new thoughts through giving them a truthful threat. Just preserve in thoughts, we've got had been given all been wrong normally and until you're willing to embrace one-of-a-kind thoughts and absolutely enjoy them you may be doomed to be wrong many more times.

The next trait that we want to embody is to emerge as an highbrow rock. What I recommend with the aid of that is that we need to emerge as on top of things of the way we see matters. Most people are ruled with the aid of manner of emotion and their views are with out trouble changed and manipulated through manner of robust feelings. Look at any of the facts channels with a political time table and you may see hyperbole and slander used as strong device to exchange minds. Even despite the fact that this actual for max human beings, it doesn't want to be so for you and me.

When we work on becoming stable as a rock intellectually we start to form our ideals not in line with emotion however consistent with commonplace sense. It takes an detail of braveness so that you can do this but we ought to be willing to evaluate and trade any and all of our ideals to in form the dictates of motive. We have to moreover be inclined to maintain those beliefs in spite of outside pressures to exchange them. This doesn't imply that we aren't willing to pay interest the arguments of others but what it does propose is that we are not going to be swayed without issues and emotionally. If our opinion is to be modified it needs to be completed thru reason as well.

The final highbrow trait to paintings on cultivating is to turn out to be honest. Becoming honest minded is a way which includes treating all viewpoints with the resource of the identical rules. Regardless of whether or not or no longer we take shipping of as true with a sure view or not, we conform to provide it a sincere threat. If we're reading the validity of a few detail that we be given as right with then we achieve this objectively trying now not to appearance exceptional for confirming evidence. This is the most tough of the highbrow tendencies but additionally one of the most essential because of the fact if we are able to discover ways to be honest-minded and impartial we are able to have taken a massive soar ahead to accurate and goal wondering. [v]

Chapter 7: Emotional intelligence and critical wondering

While no longer a essential thinking device, the capacity to have emotional intelligence is an critical praise to crucial wondering. Having the skills to logically harm down arguments and then restructure them as a cohesive entire is critical but getting to know to end up more savvy with unique humans will will let you deliver your newly logical arguments in a manner so that you can land better and make more of an impact.

If you are first rate interested in expressing mind logically then it is going to be great to bypass this financial wreck but in case you are interested by reading how you could speak your ideas efficiently then this monetary catastrophe may be a excellent beneficial useful resource for you.

"All learning has an emotional base" – Plato [vi]

The first and most critical step in enhancing your emotional intelligence is as a manner to sincerely recognize emotions. Without the capacity to 'observe human beings' the alternative abilities can be an extended way greater hard to observe. A splendid area to start for that is to learn how to spot frame language and the way to take a look at facial expressions which you can find out approximately right proper here

Once you've got determined out a way to identify the ones emotions the subsequent step is to discover ways to address the emotional points which you could tell are the most warm button subjects within the thoughts of the individual that you're talking to. If you examine that they revel in a especially sturdy emotion whenever you factor out a specific portion of your argument you then without a doubt may additionally need to do some digging to apprehend what they in reality experience approximately that idea.

The next tip is to make the character such as you by means of the usage of some old expertise from communication guru Dale

Carnegie, Namely to smile and use their name.

When you smile human beings generally tend to smile again at you. We like those who like us and smiling is the pleasant manner to carry that we just like the person we're speakme to. In addition to smiling even though, using the character's name that we Aare talking to will engender warm feelings. Carnegie even goes to date as to mention that a person's call is the sweetest sound to her or him in any language.

The remaining tip to the use of superior emotional intelligence for your communication is to learn how to control your personal horrific emotions. When you permit your emotions rule your lifestyles and at the same time as you permit your horrible emotions dominate your communique you may now not be capable of stay objective and communicate in a clear and vital way. This goes to be tremendously poor in your communications not just on a personal degree but additionally on a important questioning degree. If you're usually in a lousy mood then you'll be what the poker participant's call being "on tilt." This manner that you make horrible picks because of the fact you're emotionally roused.

Remember, within the terms of Emerson "We grow to be what we think about all day lengthy."

Chapter 8: The 4 important questioning system

Inferences

An inference is whilst we assume that due to the fact one detail is proper, odds are that the opposite is likewise true. This also can or won't be the case however they may be our first-rate strive at fact.

Compare this to an assumption, an assumption is some thing that we receive as actual with to be actual based totally completely totally on our societal and experiential beliefs. For example, if it's far assumed that Islam is a violent religion, then we'd infer that a Muslim man scowling at us way us damage but because of this misguided assumption, the inference is most possibly incorrect, he is probably searching at some element on our face or our normal style and so on... But not want to do us damage.

Synthesis

Bringing together all the relevant facts you have had been given observed that allows you to help your thesis.

Synthesis is one of the most essential gadget because of the reality it's miles at this component which you trade your information of the problem from a disorganized listing of facts, figures, and so on... and flip them right into a complete concept of what goes on on the time. When you are synthesizing you have to cause to maintain your description of the scenario as quick as viable. This will permit you to ensure that you understand the idea at a deep stage.

In the terms of Antoine de Saint-Exupery

"Perfection is completed, no longer on the identical time as there may be no longer something greater to characteristic, but on the same time as there can be not anything left to dispose of."

Implications

Implication is one of the maximum vital factors of critical thinking due to the fact being able to correctly understand what the effects of a high quality state of affairs or idea are is crucial in order no longer to make alternatives with terrible effects.

There are three kinds of implications, critical, probable, and feasible

Necessary way that if some issue takes vicinity, each different thing need to constantly have a look at from this. If I fall off of a 1000 foot building and now not the usage of a protection functions of any type I should always turn out to be drastically injured or die.

Probable manner that if event A occurs the occasion B possibly will too. If I stand on a driving variety for 1 minute at top hour, it is probable that I can be struck through way of a golfing ball.

Possible way that the risk of an implication can also furthermore arise however is not specially in all likelihood. One example is probably "If I bypass golfing then I can also additionally hit a hollow in a unmarried." Possible, but now not possibly or crucial

We need at the manner to show what we're implying, due to the reality if we mean a few aspect which isn't always actual, problems upward push up. For instance, if I make out with my pals ex-girl friend and he lets me understand that we're capable of not be pals then he's implying that he communicated effectively the concept that if I ever made out along together together with his ex's then He could not want to be buddies. If he says this at the equal time as no longer having previously set the ones expectancies then he's being unreasonable.

How to use implications

1.   country the problem you're going through

2.   brainstorm solutions

three.   write out the viable implications

four.   What form of the 3 implications are they?

Assumptions

When you count on you make an ass out of you and me!

The reality is that we need to make assumptions, because of the reality we do no longer have any experiential records of what is set to take place. If we could not make assumptions then we won't be able to consider the consequences of any given movement, we'd just ought to do it and word what takes region. When you assume that a rotting log laying across a circulate isn't steady to stroll on you are capable of make an knowledgeable bet that might prevent a few damage. Without the functionality to assume you may actually need to stroll on the log, fall in, and get moist.

So the vital issue isn't to keep away from making assumptions but if you need to pick out them with out problem and apprehend at the same time as they may be low priced and unreasonable

We need to count on some matters to be actual without evidence those proof loose statements can usually be described as "permit's suppose that..." statements. They are subjects that we are taking without any consideration. Although some quantity of assumptions are critical, be cautious of each person who makes too many assumptions or assumptions that are not usually common as possibly to be proper.

The Socratic Method

In order to demonstrate the significance of asking the proper questions so that you can stimulate suitable essential questioning and insights it's far crucial to understand one of the most notorious questioners and philosophers of all time, Socrates. Socrates become one of the fathers of contemporary-day western philosophy, he lived in Greece approximately 450 BCE and he become well-known for his approach of stimulating insight (mainly approximately ethics) which changed into referred to as the Socratic Method.

The Socratic Method have become, as you may likely guess, the way that Socrates taught. It survived his demise and has end up one of the maximum generally used and powerful strategies that a teacher can stimulate essential questioning in a pupil. It is primarily based on asking masses of questions. And other than being virtually, in reality worrying, it stimulates greater wondering than the spoon-feeding of records that we get in recent times in books and a few classrooms.

This style of education is glaringly no longer used for objective statistics or formulae very often because of the fact there are a few statistics that a student without a doubt couldn't arrive at if wondered great. The Socratic Method in fact shines thru while it's far positioned to apply approximately subjective issues like ethics or political conversations.

Although it is difficult to apply the Socratic Method yourself, it's miles a completely beneficial tool to stimulate critical thinking in buddies and own family people. This is a manner that you may get people to enter into conversations which can be definitely enlightening with out being a nuisance and irritating them. Here are a few recommendations to using the Socratic Method for your day after day life:

Keep returning to the preliminary question that you need spoke back.

One of the number one issues that you will face at the same time as the usage of the Socratic Method often is that conversations will commonly commonly generally tend to get off trouble be counted in case you are not cautious. You would probably start out speaking about your opinion at the death penalty after which abruptly discover that you are in a conversation approximately your favored music and marvel "How within the international did we get right right right here and what had been we speaking approximately besides??"

As the person that is steerage the conversation in a vital direction it's miles going to be your responsibility to hold the conversation heading in the proper path. The first problem that you are going to want to practice is without a doubt preserving the principle problem this is below talk in mind at some point of the entire verbal exchange. You will want to ensure that when the person answers one in every of your questions you remind your self of the reason of the communication through way of asking "How does what modified into definitely said relate to (insert the principle idea proper here)" By doing this you could now not only undergo in thoughts what the intention of the conversation is but you'll additionally sincerely pay interest to what's being said.

The 2nd tool which you will find out beneficial whilst the communique begins offevolved to get off route is a polite question to persuade a communication decrease back at the right song. If your pal starts offevolved to waft while speaking and goes on a bit of a tangent one splendid device which I like to use is pronouncing "Yes...and..."

For instance, if I ask about the shortage of lifestyles penalty with a friend after which they tell me a private tale about how a few modern-day crook modified into caught and the manner they think that this criminal ought to get the penalty I can also say "Oh clearly? That is virtually exciting, I will have to look at that later. Getting lower back to (insert maximum critical point proper right here)... (Insert next query right here)" This layout acknowledges what they said but it with courtesy actions the verbal exchange lower lower back to the primary concept.

Keep your questions open ended

The Socratic Method is primarily based on the approach of asking open ended questions. These are questions that could't be answered without difficulty with a yes, a no, or a truth/determine. The reason that you may need to reply open ended questions is that they'll stimulate far greater interesting and perception horrifying solutions than easy questions. If your questions may be answered with a sure or no, the percentages are that your pal will take the clean direction and do really that.

Here is the way you ensure that your questions live open ended and your conversations stay powerful, exciting, and crucial. The first manner to hold the questions open is to make sure that they may be how, and why questions. Who, what, and in which questions are typically with out issue spoke back with one or words however at the identical time as you ask how and why you questions are asking about a way and a moral judgement. These questions stimulate talk and deeper understanding than the opposite three

Another first-rate way to keep the questions open ended is to preserve topics ambiguous at the start after which get clearer because of the truth the conversational thread is going on. For example you'll likely ask on the start "Why do you think that john determined on that profession path" and then in a while say something like "Do you consider you studied that his pals affect had any impact on his profession desire" you can see that the number one query has a long way extra capability ways of answering than the second one. These are referred to as probing questions and they're tremendous for stimulating more than one answers.

Check in with what factors of the problem have and feature not been resolved.

The final method to make your use of the Socratic Method greater effective is to make certain that you preserve track of what questions have and characteristic no longer been spoke back. Usually at the same time as discussing a topic there are numerous questions a remarkable manner to return to thoughts, what the other character thinks approximately the trouble, what the different factors influencing the query must do with every one of a kind, how we must hold from proper right here information what we apprehend now, and so forth...

The exciting element about the Socratic Method is that it generates many many extra questions than distinct conversational strategies and it is simple to lose track of all of the special ideas which can be in question. Keeping all of the unique questions in thoughts and making sure that you in fact endeavor to answer they all is one of the great techniques that you may make sure which you anticipate deeply approximately the question and now not in reality considerably.

Ask "why" 5 times

The subsequent technique is known as "Ask why 5 times." Most people are acquainted with how little children will ask why again and again. "Why is the sky blue" because of the fact the sea reflects onto it "Why is the ocean blue?" Because of bacteria, algae, and minerals in it "Why are they in it?" Etc... Even even though this is frequently demanding, it is one of the reasons that children take a look at so quite rapid. What I could invite you to do is reclaim this interest thru the use of the technique on this financial disaster.

By asking why five times in a row we dive to the muse of the trouble, we discover the motives in preference to the floor manifestations of the problems.

This method become on the start decided and carried out through an employee of the Toyota motor employer. They used this approach to study why positive errors in the constructing of motors came about or to ask how they may make a system extra green. Even even though the origins of this approach have been to construct better cars and to collect vehicles extra efficaciously, we are able to use it to expect extra surely and to dive to the premise of any problem much less tough. Indeed, this questioning tool swiftly went from the Toyota motor company to many organizations, and then to the personal lives of the industrial company human beings themselves and in the long run to the network at large.

When the use of this approach it's far essential to be conscious that it leads satisfactory to at least one answer. In the actual international most issues or thoughts have multiple answer and can absolutely have many. By recognizing this vulnerable factor we're capable of learn how to use this wondering tool greater correctly. One suitable manner to do this is to ask 5 questions and then after finding a solution, do everything all all over again but search for strategies in which you could ask first-rate questions.

By finding departure factors in your thinking you can search for and discover many solutions for your preliminary query and have a better view of what an real solution could possibly appear to be.

Another aspect that we are going to need to hold in thoughts at the same time as using this approach is the tendency many people have of staying at a ground degree and not diving into the reasons. Even at the same time as asking many questions, on occasion we don't move everywhere and we don't recognize the question on a deeper degree. In order to remedy this trouble it's far important to have what I like to name "Causation recognition"

This fashion of questioning appears to locate the idea motives of a few aspect came earlier than it. When you embody causation recognition you are in essence asking yourself constantly "Is this question shifting me within the route of an information of the roots of the hassle?"

Despite the truth that the "Ask 5 questions technique" isn't excellent, it is but very useful and can be used to discover the supply of the hassle. Remember to hold in thoughts those tips, to search for the reason of the issue, and to go through the process over and over till you recognize the trouble holistically and you may be properly on the manner to the use of this device correctly.

Avoid arguments through manner of clarifying terms

In order to have a communique, people want to have the potential to speak the equal language. This truism is some issue which seems useless however how commonly have you ever ever had a conversation or an issue and it wasn't till very a ways along which you positioned out which you and the person that you were speaking to had been not on the identical internet page, you weren't speakme the identical language?

If you are something like most humans, you've got likely had this enjoy commonly, you could surely have professional it in advance in this week! Often times a subtle distinction in the expertise of a nice word or phrase will make all the difference between a efficient and clean communique and one in that you and the character you are talking to are every annoyed and harassed.

In order to combat this hassle we're going to take a pronged approach, the first is to enhance our vocabulary as an entire and the second one is to take on the addiction of asking clarifying questions

Before you discovered that enhancing your vocabulary as an entire isn't always properly worth a while I need to tell you a tale about a chum of mine. He is a top notch musician and a talented showman as nicely but up till approximately a 365 days inside the beyond his vocabulary wasn't top notch. At remaining five times an afternoon he may also want to invite what a sure phrase intended, misinterpret what I became saying, or misuse a phrase.

This result in all styles of confusion on each of our additives. Even worse, it caused many arguments. When I might accurate a poorly used word, he ought to get irritated with me, and when I used terms he didn't apprehend he got pressured and may regularly lose the thread of the communique.

After he worked to decorate his vocabulary with the beneficial resource of reading the classics and reading some philosophy (notoriously tough at the vocabulary) He and I had been capable to talk an extended manner more correctly.

In order to enhance your vocabulary I am going to signify a quicker approach than the only my pal used. This approach is a internet site which surely is aware of what terms you're gaining knowledge of and it tailors your studying to you. This net web page starts offevolved you off with as a substitute smooth phrases that any neighborhood speaker might recognize and works you into regularly tougher and extra difficult vocabulary lists. As you take a look at more and more the internet web page starts to have a observe what phrases you are statistics and what phrases you don't recognize but.

As you improvement thru the fill within the clean and more than one desire questions vocabulary.Com will maintain tune of your improvement in a improvement bar which accompanies every word. Once you are very advanced in a phrase vocabulary.Com will ask you much less and much less questions about that word. When you have proven a entire facts of a phrase it leaves the everyday rotation of the terms you are getting to know and it enters a listing off terms which you have mastered. These mastered phrases are most effective requested approximately as soon as every few months.

The 2d manner that you can make clear what is meant and make certain which you and the person with whom you are speakme are on the equal web page is to ask clarifying questions These questions are treasured at the same time as you're speaking approximately a completely technical trouble or your are speakme about some thing that is very subjective like someone's emotions or evaluations.

One manner to recognize which phrases you want to make clean are is to look for habitual terms, what it that the person says over and over is. They might also say "They clearly make me so warm beneath the collar" or "I in reality can't placed my thumb on it." These idiomatic expressions are frequently indistinct and surely hard to recognize however with the resource of manner of understanding to search for them and make clean them you will be able to better apprehend wherein the individual you're speaking to is coming from.

Compared to the thoughts that we learned in the section at the Socratic Method which taught us the way to invite open ended questions, those questions have that allows you to be responded in a short and clean manner. These questions want to be capable of be resolved with a reality, a determine, a call, a easy fine or no, and so forth...

We need to work to ask the open ended questions first with a view to get an expansive and massive information of what we're talking approximately but then you can need to invite clarifying inquiries to hone in on precisely what is meant. A key takeaway proper here is if you can't solution your private questions with a easy reality or determine, you then definitely definately need to artwork to make clear the problem otherwise it's going to grow to be growing ambiguity inside the verbal exchange and making choice greater tough than it wants to be.

Chapter 9: Make positive that you have a purpose

In addition to all the thoughts that we've looked at up to now, we ought to increase our purpose in conversation. It is super to recognise approximately logical fallacies, strategies of uncovering what's at the muse of an trouble, highbrow necessities and dispositions and so on… but with out a cause, a verbal exchange has a bent to wander and neither party goes to be satisfied with the final results. Without a motive inside the returned of our questioning we are able to have a propensity to get distracted and spend greater time than crucial on any given idea or problem that we are going thru. Without a smooth motive, we cannot be able to exercising essential thinking

How are you capable of find out the purpose of a few component it is that you are considering?

The procedure of bobbing up with a cause is a hard however worthwhile one. Here are some beneficial questions if you want to help you to recognize why you are running on the concept in query:

Am I seeking out a solution for myself or for someone else?

Often instances we're capable of struggle with defining our purpose due to the fact we fail to recognise that the purpose in the back of our inquiry isn't for ourselves but for our instructors, or our employers. If this is the case, it's far essential to ask your self what that man or woman needs from your artwork and then to deliver paintings which meets their expectancies.

What will be the excellent outcome of this inquiry?

When you are reading a paper or wearing out a communication or working through an issue on your mind it is treasured to assume the fine feasible outcome of the scenario. You may think what the outstanding end cease end result of a marital dispute may be, or what the nugget of information is which you are seeking out to extract is from a book.

What moves do I want to be taken after this?

If you are writing a persuasive letter or talking with a friend or considering how you could beautify the fantastic of your life, it will likely be beneficial to recollect what moves you want to appearance because of the vital thinking method. Remember that the critical wondering method isn't some thing that stays absolutely within the thoughts however it additionally turns into an movement inside the actual international.

When thinking about what moves you want to appearance, ask yourself the way you need your buddy, worker, partner, to act because of the inquiry which you are placing ahead.

When asking this query of yourself, don't forget how a higher model of yourself ought to act on the statistics which you are studying because of the inquiry.

Understanding and use your reading fashion

Although no longer strictly related to critical questioning, statistics your gaining information of favor will will allow you to digest the raw statistics that critical wondering is primarily based on a wonderful deal much less hard. Understanding the manner you study brilliant will help you in all regions of your existence however because it pertains to critical thinking it's miles going to be most beneficial at the identical time as you are on the lookout for to accumulate data (do not forget that phase of the device?)

Most human beings don't understand that we absolutely analyze in one-of-a-kind processes and that a style of getting to know that works for one person is probably nearly impossible to look at from for each different character. This is critical to recognize because of the reality in the long run the awesome of your wondering is decided with the aid of your ability to build up and understand information.

There are 3 vital types of studying that everybody has. We are all capable of analyze the usage of all of these structures however there's normally one device which is going high-quality. These 3 structures are the visible, the auditory, and the bodily style. (Kinesthetic)

The seen learner...

Learns exquisite from graphs and seen demonstrations. They can take a look at peoples facial expressions and frame language in an uncannily accurate manner. They possibly respect video excellent, exquisite photos, lovely art work, and many others... If they are in a lecture or searching an informative speech they may will be inclined to keep their eyes professional on the speaker in area of looking on the slides or at their notes.

The auditory learner

Tends to look down at their notes while taking them. Tends to be aware about the tone of voice greater than watch the body language. Enjoys stay indicates and taking note of track. Enjoys and can have a look at nicely from audiobooks.

The kinesthetic learner....

The physical learner has a bent to analyze exceptional in arms on environment, they'll be the sort of man or woman who is probably succesful to expose you the manner they do something with out having the ability to tell you absolutely how they did it. They will generally be fantastic at generation or math or each. They have a knack for reading physical capabilities and is probably an athlete.

Now which you understand these three varieties of learning, which might be you? Identify this as short as feasible and strive to check to your most snug modality as frequently as possible any similarly. I for one am an auditor learner and now I look at almost totally thru audiobooks or YouTube motion photos gambling within the history as I pass approximately my day. Understanding my gaining knowledge of fashion has taken my records of the fabric drastically and in case you understand your gaining expertise of fashion you may watch your know-how of numerous subjects shoot up in a single day. [vii]

Critical wondering tick list

This listing is loosely primarily based mostly on the college of Sussex checklist

Identify the important stuff.

What are the vital element mind, arguments, and conclusions?

What is the evidence?

Evaluate the findings

Is the proof considerable sufficient to purpose the perception?

What assumptions and inferences are being made implicitly or explicitly?

Is there any research this is relevant, updated, and that backs up the conclusion?

Is the common experience sturdy? Are there any logical fallacies or leaps in common sense which might be unfounded?

How is emotion being used? Is it biased or does it simply have a place?

Look beyond to the consequences

What are a few particular viewpoints that we may not were thinking about?

How does your earlier information relate to these thoughts?

What are the results of what you have got got been analyzing, thinking about, speaking approximately, or being attentive to?

Develop a clean issue of view.

Sum up the statistics

Synthesize it

Draw low priced conclusions

Be capable of articulate your aspect of view steady with the fucking intellectual requirements.

Chapter 10: Why Is Critical Thinking Important?

Basic Ideology

Critical Thinking is called the analytical approach for developing a judgment. It is what separates rational wondering from irrational wondering. Yet, on the equal time, it is a more polished model of rational assessment. A verdict/assertion that comes out of your thoughts through four ranges of processing: not unusual feel, evidence, observational assessment, and personal studies on the given problem. Each degree holds its degree of significance, and this can be a few aspect that we may be addressing absolutely in monetary disaster variety of the ebook.

There may be loads of misconceptions concerning important wondering. For example, a few human beings fathom important thinking as a capability that is possible with the aid of exceptionally knowledgeable professors or folks that are considered luminaries in their respective fields on my own. Their faulty assumption can also country that vital questioning is viable for people who own an excellent quantity of desired knowledge. Though education and global expertise offers an person a large gain, my personal studies say otherwise. For me, the precept origins of essential evaluation will commonly come from cleaning one's haughty character. Why? It is because of the truth the arena is full of infinite resources of records. A man can educate himself from the very first days of learning to look at and write until loss of existence takes him. Yet, even then, he's certain to leave at the back of an ok quantity of know-how that he should in no way studies approximately.

My cardinal component of emphasis being is the capability of studying extra ultra-modern subjects as life includes you to massive possibilities. As long as a person is following the simple rituals of his / her instructional lifestyles, they will grow to be smarter and additional smart. However, even in case you had been to achieve the very mountain top and earned a doctorate for yourself (Ph.D.), your efforts in becoming greater seriously charged might be futile because of the lack of information inner you. What saddens me is that such people do virtually inhabit our planet.

They are well identified, well informed, and do maintain in mind themselves as beings of spreading coherent messages. However, hypocrisy involves moderate whilst the ones very equal people pass on racist, stereotypical, sacrilegious, and acerbic feedback inside the route of human beings of numerous beliefs/cultures. Just like lust is the eradicator of affection, keeping grudges and having an egotistical personality is the demolisher of vital questioning. Taming one's stubbornness and accomplishing higher necessities of morality is what you want to become a critical truth seeker.

As the well-known quote says, "Virtue starts offevolved from domestic."

History / Origin

Logics and guidelines of the universe that appear too smooth to recognize and take a look at these days have been as fast as misplaced secrets and techniques and techniques. After all, even the pull of gravity force life became no longer diagnosed till an apple fell on Newton's head. Critical questioning has really a similar gist whilst we talk approximately its origins. Etymology, regarding the primary account ever positioned for vital wondering, dates once more to loads of years in the beyond.

Leading decrease returned to ancient Greece, wherein Socrates have become the number one philosophical man to apprehend the want for implementing critical wondering in certainly all of us. A term wherein human beings believed in the electricity of an expert figurehead to make the wisest of alternatives, as you may choose for yourself, this idea lacked each not unusual sense in addition to reasoning.

Socrates debated on it and expressed how actual belief can't come from a higher hierarchy on my own. A character's fame in no way links to rational wondering Instead, a justification must be reached through manner of questioning outdoor the field for as soon as. Subjects of debate and selection making must be tackled with the unique tiers that we noted at the begin of the chapter. Socrates helped to pierce commonplace stereotypical beliefs of human beings which have been immoral to speak approximately upon earlier than. Opening gateways to innovation and better mindsets

Significance

Where to begin? The essence of important wondering surrounds each and each way of life that we abide in. May it is our love existence, artwork-existence, or definitely the regular hustle. When we contemplate over the notion of a like minded couple, their sustainability of creating their relationship artwork is based totally carefully upon having the first-rate of thinking critically.

If now not in every, then as a minimum in one in every of them if no longer, there will normally be pitfalls in terms of statistics each extraordinary's manner of living. There can be judgments made that do not even crack the floor of every other's personalities. Not to mention, in terms of fights, each will live oblivious to every exclusive's flaws. Thus, it's far going to be a combat to earn that egotistical pleasure alone. Every strength couple to be had determined important wondering to interpret their companion to his / her fullest. Letting them verify every and each new section of their love lifestyles with sensibility and proper capability. One of the maximum tough dilemmas for newlyweds to art work around is managing their monetary stability. Critical wondering will assist them in springing up with a sly charge variety that fulfills all of the requirements wanted alongside a few savings. It may also be used to talk about jogging situations. If every the partners are going for walks people, they will manage to discover that center floor in which they may be capable of offer their whole interest with out disrupting their workflow simultaneously.

Efficiency and effectiveness are the 2 pillars of a hit work existence. Both key factors this is bland with out the addition of crucial thinking or evaluation. Efficiency is the amount of output you can positioned on a desk, while effectiveness is the quantity to which a person is able to achieving the quality (or above) outcomes. Critical thinking to your paintings defines your passion and your degree of interest to find out higher techniques to surpass others and intention for that big advertising. At the same time, performance is right away proportional to someone's time control talents.

A higher maintain near on time technique getting greater paintings finished at a smaller length. Critical wondering will assist in creating a properly-rounded time desk a good way to feature on; a time table that safeguards the crowning glory of each obligatory purpose along leisure time. Lastly, the importance of critical thinking on your art work lifestyles moreover may be a responsibility. The most primary instance that includes mind is a clinical physician, engineer, and a detective.

A nurse or a health care employer will brainstorm their minds to offer the most appropriate and appropriate deal with their patients. Whether it is selecting their remedy, amount of mattress rest wanted, and developing with the very last verdict of what a person is virtually laid low with. This is classified through a sequence of complicated assessments, assessment of the affected person's scientific information, and their expertise of biology.

After all, it can be a count of lifestyles and dying. An engineer carefully chooses the proper amount and shape of substances desired an notable manner to form the foundation of a building. Good engineering results in safety from herbal disasters which includes earthquakes. Lastly, in ordinary life, our mind is usually challenged to speak its reviews over worldly subjects. Critical questioning does no longer make you 100% correct. No you may despite the fact that attain that sort of perfection, however it does offer you with remarkable apprehend and energy to stand up for your logical reasoning. No you likely can near your voice while it's far had to be heard.

Whatever the conundrums possibly, your essential wondering will assist lay stepping stones in the direction of their solutions.

Productivity, quandary dissolving, raising a particular voice the diverse not unusual crowd, becoming extra mentally huge wide awake, and installing place the independence of your flaws and proficiencies are the advantages of enforcing critical thinking.

Chapter 11: Fundamental Concepts Of Critical Thinking.

Every revolutionizing device or idea that humanity has encounter is a mixture of multiple factors. Greatest thoughts are a mixture of youngster factors much like a meals recipe. Critical wondering is definitely the equal, whether or not or now not or no longer we label it as levels, additives, elements, or thoughts. In financial disaster one, we delivered into consciousness the overall terminology of critical thinking, its historic background in addition to its importance.

Those who have never heard of essential wondering could not fathom the amount of self-checking that is going into arranging desirable judgment with idea. Then linking perception with an commentary and remark with history data. Then via connecting know-how with rhetoric phrases to finish a number one pattern of essential questioning.

It ought to in all likelihood look like a large system however our human thoughts is in a function sufficient to do it in a rely of seconds, if we are willing enough. Remember, Critical wondering is that channel of higher popularity that undertakes any topic of dialogue or communication and allows you be that one unique voice in a collection of chatter. Improving the overall exceptional of your thinking, the communique and captivating the lesser minds round you altogether. So what are the ones important thoughts of vital questioning that coalesce to mold the capability of our thinking tiers.

Logic

If we have been to erase the foundation / basis of any infrastructure spherical us, then what is going to be the inevitable cease? The constructing can be certain to fall, for the very base that held it high and robust is now no more. Moreover, if a chef chefs his fowl underneath the best enough temperature, what do you finish from that situation as properly? The chicken may be undercooked, risking each his customer's fitness and his popularity within the culinary corporation.

What facilitates us arrive to those impetuous but accurate solutions? It is "not unusual experience," proper? Logic technique assessing some element with already-mounted validity. Due to this very truth, common sense is the primary essential concept of crucial thinking. Detecting the provision of proper judgment in all and sundry's desire of terms may be the initial comments from our thoughts. Again, count on logically. What is there to don't forget critically if the difficulty in hand is as a whole, fatuous. Critical wondering is not pretty tons comprehending problems with the aid of the usage of questioning out of doors the sphere. By thinking appreciably you'll prevent yourself from indulging in topics for you to first-class lead you closer to wastage of treasured time.

You will understand in which your certainly clearly really worth of thoughts is certainly needed and wherein it isn't. Availability of commonplace experience will then at once click on your mind to dig deeper and waft onto the following be conscious-well worth concept: rhetoric.

Being Rhetorical

Rhetoric approach the usage of verbal language this is cajoling and spellbinding enough to make your terms greater influential to the listener. A clean instance may be of the addition of a condiment in any dish that wishes it. Excluding any from the dish will bring about what type of taste? A bland one, reliant on the flavour of the substances themselves. The majority of the flavor of the dish will display to be bland and abysmal. Consider being rhetoric due to the reality the spice of essential wondering. You can display yourself to be as logical and informed enough as you need to but your phrases will fall brief with out the brought kick of rhetoric.

People want to abuse the concept of being rhetoric via consisting of the element of exaggeration. However, critical thinking glaringly dismisses this. You can beautify your charismatic (rhetoric) wondering via the use of the usage of hand gestures (on occasion called gesticulation). Hand gestures are labeled as non-verbal technique of communication and their reason is to extend the overall attraction of verbal communication. The tone of your voice is going an extended manner as nicely. A prevented and shy voice will in no manner be inviting for folks who need to be happy or proved wrong. Instead, actual firmness and determination in a single's is what ignites a certain degree of interest in every body inside the paying attention to variety.

Some may additionally additionally moreover even call it being philosophical. However, essential questioning isn't alleged to be as ambiguous and vague as poetry, or philosophy. Its schedule wants to be sharp and without issues visible to oldsters which can be paying attention. Perfect this and you will without issue impose your very own however precise specific judgment inside the the front of folks which are too baffled to fathom it and update it with their non-public notion.

Observation

You may additionally have learnt the essentiality of assertion in technological expertise. Without announcement, scientists can by no means go with the waft onto venture experiments. Observations are a key aspect that facilitates a scientist acquire sufficient facts to definitely touch upon it. This permits the researcher to then placed his findings to a sensible use. Critical thinking adopts the very same attitude of announcement. Once the commonplace sense is decided, the statistics following common experience want to be taken into consideration. For example, someone claims to be properly informed about his understanding concerning extremely good non secular beliefs.

However, his mind and terms tackling the problem come off as stereotypical and media-driven. To be extra specific, his so referred to as expertise isn't his very very own personal research. The man or woman is absolutely quoting the misconceptions established in films, serials and fake media of television. All of this could be judged via your diploma of observation. In truth, statement is probably the powerhouse of your critical questioning. Focusing on the information of what will make you agree with you studied are precisely what are going to make it important as properly.

Observation desires the detail of criticality as well. Observation concerned right here must be vigilant enough to word even the most tiniest and diffused greater info.

You ought to start to be conscious the body language and tone of every person you have interaction with, to the factor of it becoming a unconscious assertion; bear in thoughts it your sixth sense. Through this you'll constantly see a person's real sun shades and rationale. You will benefit foresight to any malice or hidden time table someone can also own, and guard your self in the system.

Connect the why, how and while along facial expressions, verbal tone and the preceding impressions made thru particular a person. Bad observation can be able to disrupting your personal photo of accurate judgment and cardinal aspect toward which you in the end plan to attain. It is like going for walks out the fine steps of a numerical and yet writing down a incorrect answer within the easy of a mathematics test. Room for fecklessness and haste isn't an opportunity without a blink of a doubt.

Argumentative Analysis

Now we come to the essential idea of important thinking. The very baking oven of vital wondering one may also want to say. Though we're going to be discussing arguments and a manner to deal with them in financial disaster 3, we can not brush aside its massive significance as a essential idea of essential thinking as properly. So how precisely do you breakdown an difficulty from the opposition detail (the argument does now not necessarily want to return from an opposition)? It is all in the amount of options you could deliver to yourself so that you can discover the individual's attitude and widen your viewing lens.

The first step is to divide the argument into its most important subjects. Is it completely highlighting one factor of interest or does it further increase alongside? Look for contradicting perspectives. Contradicting views characterize an ordinary susceptible argument with out a solid authenticity. Moreover, arguments can be a combination of each facts in addition to critiques.

If each arguments emerge as considered as statistics, the realization you'll advantage together at the side of your important questioning might be false. Similarly, if with the useful resource of mistake, you expect each as reviews, then this is carelessness as properly. Your final judgment in regards to the argument's give up will come from the primary evidence provided and the tone of the person making the argument. Did he stop with a super reinforcement or bad reinforcement? The argument may even stop at a independent nation. Your response will reflect to your analytical competencies.

A particular reaction will cope with the argument from all viable pointers. It will now not be one sided besides in truth important. It will pinpoint suitable and awful statements made through the other person. It will decide the authenticity and the know-how of the speaker as properly. Any plot holes ought to be absolutely mentioned and tackled as nicely.

Lastly, the series of your reaction has its private influential impact. Your assessment might be better favored if you comply with a chronological order. Discussing each hassle with a extra moderen assertion and backing it up with effective evidences and rhetoric speech.

Reasoning with Probabilities and Data

Just how close to fact is someone's views? Are they powerful elements and but seem farfetched or they're as an alternative easy however the hazard of them being right is quite excessive? This little brain teaser is a few factor you will want to get used to. However, the exceptional statistics is that in case you're well informed approximately the concern being debated upon, then your history information will pretty a terrific deal act as a threat meter. A critical truth seeker is not a wannabe. He or she knows whilst to manner in and on the same time as to remain at a distance. We attention on the trouble on which we sincerely can dominate and feature our voices heard.

Therefore, avoid becoming worried in an issue on the manner to risk your private popularity. Ensure to perform enough studies on the scenario earlier than starting to debate with a person.

If I end up to get into an problem with a person among a topic I actually have end up properly-observe in, such as philosophy, my hazard of assessing the concern to its furthest limits could be better. My reasoning might be sponsored up with intimidating replies along their easy evidences as well. No one walks proper into a conflict region without a firearm. In a warfare of important questioning, your historical past expertise is what enables you guard your castle.

Critical thinking is all approximately connecting the dots to non-ambiguous verdicts. Knowledge isn't quite a lot imprinting an encyclopedia on your mind. Knowledge is available in all office work as we flow alongside in life. It comes from beyond activities of our non-public non-public lives in addition to history.

Earlier I referred to that no man can ever absolutely educate himself the everlasting knowledge of the arena we live in. It is continuously wiser to observe as you circulate along. Staying desk certain is to boycott your self from residing newer escapades in lifestyles. This in move back evolves your mind to assume greater proficiently, improving the dexterity of your functionality to contemplate. Self-deceiving, like everyday, isn't always an opportunity. Unconscious prejudice can constantly stay part of us. Keeping it in check and making sure that it does not get cooked up with our actual feedback is a take a look at for our maturity.

The functionality to self-actualize and refine our prone spots does now not have a completing line. If you bear in mind you studied otherwise, then you definately surely are falling prey to an egotistical mindset.

Logic, being rhetoric, observation, argumentative evaluation and threat in keeping with ancient beyond understanding is what gives beginning essential thinking. Just like a water cycle, those vital ideas need to offer constantly to modify a natural system inner.

"The essence of the impartial thoughts lies no longer in what it thinks, but in the way it thinks." ~ Christopher Hitchens.

As mentioned within the introduction of the e-book, we stay in an technology wherein there can be an incessant warfare of cultures taking place in each route of the globe. Let your thoughts do some unique. A crowd of a hundred ignorant haters can be cured via manner of a single, but super critical philosopher.

Chapter 12: What Makes An Argument Good Or Bad, And How To Construct A Good Argument?

An argument refers to reasoning with a rely that advocates its recognition or implementation. Perks of being a vital logician consists of the potential to distinguish amongst a coherent and outstanding argument and an illogical argument that effects in no understandable stop. It is steady to say that such a skills can permit someone to growth his / her effectiveness in lifestyles (as cited in financial ruin one) along their self notion as well.

Effectiveness is the amount within the direction of which you can do a little component with satisfactory or above-commonplace performance. Effectiveness can be accomplished to both engaging in a venture in addition to you make a decision. Being decisive and accurate in existence is a number one hack. If we had been to peek into our past, then it's miles pretty apparent that anybody have made horrible picks, whether or not we had been too extra youthful on the time, much less informative, or clearly misled.

On the alternative hand, human mistakes is part of realism. We cannot overlook approximately our tendency to make errors. As Shakespeare says, "to err is to be human." However, we are able to truly decrease the opportunities of human mistakes immensely, and essential thinking is important to this. Therefore, how are we able to look into arguments in our every day lives? How can we label them as unique, terrible, and discover ways to shape our very very own? All it takes are a few key elements to preserve onto tenaciously as you preserve residing your lifestyles. Rest is the attraction of critical thinking.

Let your decisiveness advantage more precision so you can also are living thru life greater easily with lesser 2nd mind. Sit once more and clear up a few clean pointers to conform so that you may enhance your outlook on arguments.

Bad Arguments

In exceptional terms, an wonderful supply of losing every person's precious time; those who fail to find out terrible argument can end up not only losing their time but also can face the effects that come because of that terrible argument. Hence, the super way to do that is through breaking down the argument. Something that we may be doing for specific arguments as properly, it makes the entire argument much less complex and much less enigmatic to apprehend.

• Ambiguity and vagueness are essential population of a horrific argument. From head to toe, you could not be results able to decide the speaker's element of view. A part of you may make you question your competency of crucial thinking; however, once you switch out to be greater professional in differentiating, you may now not blame yourself.

The root cause might be pretty smooth, certainly. Such a motive for a lousy argument can also be categorized as a logical fallacy. A logical fallacy may be located whilst the realization of an trouble does not be a part of the dots with the proof, examples, and know-how it modified into derived from, this means that that the entire imperative a part of the argument modified into invalid to what got here out as a conclusion.

• Lack of private research is a few different supply of spotting a awful argument. Signs of prone studies in an issue can be pinpointed thru the records and evidences supplied through the speaker. Are they scientific, proved by way of manner of outstanding minds, or are they stereotypical and driven off from unauthentic articles on social media? Any argument this is primarily based definitely totally on a stereotypical, racist, grudge or social media nonsense want to be labeled as a vulnerable argument automatically. These are toxic inclinations of a controversy for you to by no means cause a substantial end.

• Contemplating the change that the modern-day argument will bring with it. Is it favored or no longer? Would it effect others as a pleasing reinforcement? Will it question their art work safety? Basically, you may be studying the "motive and effect" of any such controversy spherical you. Such questions need to freely go together with the drift approximately your head whilst assessing a controversy from all guidelines.

• If the concept is made on a destiny trend and is subsidized with a effective records that helps the outcome of that argument in a few way, even then, this type of controversy is simplest an assumption. It may additionally possibly need extra precise revision or hobby.

Good Arguments

Good arguments have lifted each philosopher, reality seeker, poet, artist, baby-kisser, or even the common man from their seats of comfort. To enhance and are searching for answers whose well worth have to result in alternate according with their perspectives and know-how, Although the element of human errors can in no way sincerely go away, mastering the expertise to signify a controversy as, "desirable," can clearly purpose better choice making.

A proper argument covers all key factors. Some may additionally prove to be weaker than others. For instance, the evidence is probably sturdy, however the evaluation on it can have used extra warm temperature. The cardinal component being is that an wonderful argument is a fulfillment in being persuasive to its audience through giving heed to each situation remember of hobby with excessive excellent key factors which includes:

• A actual argument constantly follows the advocated structure. Something that we can supply into attention in bankruptcy amount four as properly. A accurate argument made with the aid of a person, no matter how intimidating, can usually mold itself inside the most convenient shape viable. A correct argument honestly observes the situation. Begs to are searching out its proof and then backs it up with powerful rhetorical sentences to installation its authenticity.

• It's easy of any kind of fallacies. Especially logical fallacies, now not like in terrible arguments. Not to mention, all the elements are met with mature motives that offer no offense to all people/a few issue.

• Quality equals sufficiency. Meaning, that a splendid argument is not dragged nor does it fall short in its nicely worth and which means. It is flawlessly stated that it'd not allow a whole lot of doubts to be raised. Bad arguments, alternatively, ought to have none of these elements or probable one. Never each!

• The well-known Straw guy fallacy is considered quite unprofessional and need to be, in all technique, not noted and now not considered as a reasonably-priced tactic to undermine the spirit of your opponent. Straw man's technique relies on weakening your opponent's component of the story on cause. Making one's argument seems stupid and decided for interest-on the lookout for. It might be terrible to at least one's recognition as a important truth seeker. Symbolizing him or her as fraud and bringing the stigma in order to get related on the factor of it.

• Good arguments are further reinforced through manner of powerful opposition as properly. It would in all likelihood seem like a massive gamble; however, in case you are a hit in repelling and disproving such objections, your argument will rework into being 3 times more exhilarating.

• Confidence. Now there may be a distinction among being assured and to also be ignorant. I say self assurance incredible for folks who are well assured of their skills in making arguments due to enjoy. They should live confident that allows you to channel the gut feeling. This will, in move decrease returned, cause better selection making and higher argument implementation.

Constructing A Good Argument

Now we clearly mingle with the cons of a awful argument and experts of an tremendous argument. You now non-public the fundamental expertise as to what makes a selection the creditability of an issue. Portray your questioning first and then permit it map out the appropriate name for interest in the direction of your important argument. From there onwards, provide concrete-sturdy proofs that'll convey your "unique" argument via the objections.

Answer as many as possible to enhance the overall authenticity of your argument. If you're already valid to your arguments in addition to vital questioning, leave no room for being cynical. Confidence is that adrenaline that urges you to pay attention to your gut feeling. Studies have proven that the primary idea that enters our mind has an inclination to be the proper one. The fear of failure or being wrong want to be kicked outside the window for errors that make us encompass humility. They help us gain extra moderen heights in lifestyles via manner of the usage of patching up the errors made within the beyond. The kingdom of being a vital logician is ever-evolving, and your capacity to growth positive arguments should not fall too an extended manner from the tree as nicely.

As a ways as I in reality have observed, maximum important thinkers will be predisposed to be introverts as nicely. I am, of direction, discussing the younger age here.

They are taciturn specifically because of the fact that no individual might certainly undertaking their degree of mind. This is in no way being haughty nor egotistical. Just one of the traits an introvert can very very own. Hence, my focal factor being, that socializing will gain you substantially. Keep putting out with buddies and try to meet extra moderen papers, you could remedy poverty, most cancers, and obtain worldwide peace in mind. Learn to represent them in a verbal way as well with the proper fusion of argument's tone.

Moreover, using hand gestures and frame movement may be a amazing addition too. Words can achieve this a whole lot as to offer an purpose of, but placing the overall surroundings of searching popularity is in your fingers on my own. Worst case scenario? A character with a terrible argument need to turn out to be dominating the primary level. "Yeah, we cannot allow that take place now, can we?" my largest advice to you will be to no longer take part in each to be had argument. How to apprehend if an problem really calls for your interest? It will cajole you in the route of it, receive as actual with me. In all honesty, arguments are mentally laborious, and now and again they require you to provide extra intake than it's far required. This might be because of robust objections or a skeptical goal market.

The rest of the chapter pretty lots falls decrease again to its importance. Like Margaret Heffernan has stated in one of her most praiseworthy prices, "For right thoughts and real innovation, you want human interplay, struggle, argument, and debate."

Chapter 13: How To Write A Good Argumentative Essay?

Critical questioning is a pedestal of intellectual degree, wherein locating our manner spherical one-of-a-type situations and its outcomes are just a beginning. The functionality to be reflective thru ours and one-of-a-kind man or woman's moves and personality furthermore embodies the factors of crucial thinking. As kids, we had been taught a way to create a comparison amongst what is right and what is wrong. Critical questioning expands on that very same workout and allows us to construct concrete-strong arguments for positive reasoning.

Followed through the usage of the concepts we cited in financial disaster and the elements examined in financial damage 3, bankruptcy four isn't always approximately identifying and fathoming the origins of an trouble in play. Chapter four is about writing it down within the most fascinating manner possible.

The following financial ruin will will can help you draft an essay that incites even the skeptics to for as quickly as ponder on some component apart from their very very own gadgets of regulations. If we appearance lower returned on the description of the e-book, I raised a question. "Every extraordinary thoughts has valued the energy of a pen and speech over nuclear weaponry. Yet, what's the ammunition of effective phrases?" Followed with the beneficial aid of a proper away answer, "critical wondering." Imagine if they had handiest notion about such mind and in no manner stricken to write down down them down. We will don't have any account or proper source via which it could have been assessed that essential wondering is the real ammunition of a pen.

If you are capable of thinking notably, then you definately need to be able sufficient to explicit it on a piece of paper. A tangible asset of essential wondering will continuously be greater treasured and actual. Otherwise, nowadays, we want to have categorized any set of writing that added positive adjustments with a random name.

So how do you provide that extraordinary structural alignment for your argumentative essay? Everything that would come off as complicated will become a lot less complicated whilst damaged down into much less difficult steps. That is how we are going to undertake the mastering of writing an argumentative essay. It can be a mixture of the primary argument further to objections. A real analytical masterpiece, you can research. If we begin from scratch, mainly, we usually have three bodies of an argumentative essay.

The Good Old Introductory, Main And Concluding Sections

In extraordinary terms, we will label it due to the fact the start, the middle, and the give up. These 3 headings, if stored in mind, assist in splitting up our essay into an unblemished form that's freed from any type of fallacy. One of the largest moments of foolishness that is linked with an argumentative essay is that people tend to underestimate the essence of the initial paragraph in their essay.

These are the phrases which might be going to persuade the reader into getting hooked with interest as to what is to come back returned inside the main segment of your essay. Being rhetoric is one of the remarkable approaches to make your advent more alluring and attractive for the pastimes of the reader.

However, rhetorical sentences can frequently reason exaggeration and additional data. Not for as soon as, ought to you overlook approximately that this is wherein you may be introducing your target market to the precept argument. The very center of interest that needs to be deciphered as you moves along.

Thus, do no longer lessen the entry of your thesis by means of manner of spending too prolonged on ambiguous and vague sentences. A properly-sharpened argumentative essay usually tackles the precept argument as fast as feasible. Tackling the argument itself can be executed in a rhetorical way. However, the extension of your argument must stay under sensible limitations.

For example, if my argumentative essay have become going to spotlight the inclined aspects of our police pressure, then I will now not linger my phrases around one of a kind economic and government-associated feebleness of my u.S.. Think about it. Those could be one in all a kind arguments as properly, and this is exactly why you must refrain from such styles of writing. This is amongst number one fallacies if I can also additionally upload. If we had been to divert the thoughts of our readers with more recent exceptional arguments, the number one argument may want to lose its middle meaning. This consequences in no impact of seeking to achieve this or trade taking location in the coronary heart of your target marketplace. Finding that ideal balance among relevancy, the primary difficulty, and a serene tone that foreshadows what is but to come again later is what an outstanding introduction is all about. If we were talking about a crucial evaluation of Robert Frost's poetry, perhaps then I would possibly have endorsed this sort of pattern. However, even then as an ardent reader of literature, I can assure you that no argument is supposed to be stretched.

Main Body

The main frame of your argumentative essay is in which all of the mind, assumptions, and cardinal factors will come into writing. Introduction phase introduced your essential argument, on the equal time as over proper right here, you may ultimately elaborate on it.

What separates the number one section of a easy essay and an argumentative essay? It is the insertion of objections. While a clean essay keeps on its manner one-way street sample, an superb argumentative essay introduces objections as well. The objection is an problem this is going in opposition to your fundamental argument in the essay. Its cause is to accentuate as to why your most important argument additionally can be examined as a terrible argument. Objections in an essay help in having a greater persuasive tone. It urges the reader/goal market to count on more deeply.

They'll be contemplating on the question, as to what is going to your end issue with? Will you be siding along side your vital argument anyhow or pick out the objection's aspect of the tale? If you are new to reading argumentative essays, this might truely baffle you. The concept of prevailing your argument and but furthermore objecting it's miles difficult. However, this is the way it want to be completed. Since, to make a reader do not forget, their mentality wants to be driven into attention from all factors of your most crucial argument. An argumentative essay with out objection is pretty sincere, and it'll come off as you attempting to steer people into growing a blind perception for the side of the tale you consider is actual. Normally, others will endorse you to insert susceptible objections on your argumentative essay. A inclined objection is a element this is going toward your argument, however it is pretty easy to disprove with proper statistics and common experience.

However, if you in truth want to be a robust argumentative essay creator, I will advise using strong objections, which beg for strong replies as well. The purpose inside the returned of this is straightforward. Weak objections are less difficult to disprove due to the truth the expertise had to collect this is quite primary. Such objections will now not spotlight you need a completely unique logician. It will paintings for an target market who is certainly oblivious in that recall. However, if the audience is properly knowledgeable and includes skeptics, then strong objections are your way to go to. A strong objection can be met with extra powerful proof and historical records assessments to further outline the authenticity of your most important argument. This will permit your essay to achieve the volume of a skeptic's interests also.

A short instance to sum up everything may be an emphasis on cutting-edge-day schooling device. If your argument urges the reader that college policies want to be changed, then your objection/objections should address the already present regulations of schools, which might be in reality beneficial. For instance, the way subject is installed and controlled in instructional institutes. A counterpoint to this objection might be the massive load artwork and stress that is positioned upon the young soul's shoulders at this type of younger age.

The gist of what I am trying to put into effect right here want to be clean thru now. Know your target market and form the strength of your objection according with that.

Conclusion (Reply)

The conclusion of your objection will pretty plenty kingdom that the objection is weakly built and falls short in phrases of idea and complete acknowledgment. The end of your respond will then aspect with the primary argument that overshadows the objection given above.

The concluding degree of your essay can all over again gain from rhetoric speech. A fashionable vibe of a decisive surrender is what you want to achieve in it. A mini recap of all that you have referred to can be given a perception as nicely. The final piece fits in an entire puzzle, in the end. By combining the introductory section, crucial argument, objection, respond, and cease, we acquire 5 systems that form an argumentative essay.

Many, at this point, question one aspect often. "Is it obligatory to comply with this sample?" Yes, it is endorsed which you gain this, but it isn't always a compulsion. If we had been to encompass such restrictive guidelines in writing as nicely, then it truely is in truth barbaric. A one-of-a-kind pattern can embody more than one premise of your primary argument. Each is then dealt with its separate objection and settled with a respond. It may additionally complicate matters, however some essays do call for a web of diverse premises and objections. For now, abide thru the simple pattern and allow your reminiscences in argumentative essay writing carry you to greater moderen and further concept-provoking patterns.

Common Mistakes When Writing an Argumentative Essay

1.   Not staying heading inside the proper course is the only of errors made thru newbie writers. This is not a fault of your crucial questioning abilties. It's a easy human errors that can be dedicated in the midst of being persuasive and argumentative.

This is something we mentioned at the very beginning of the primary subheading of this financial disaster. The super answer: the practice is more than enough enough. Always open together with your most effective viewpoints and hold onto to them tenaciously for the duration of the essay (do now not be repetitive). Your brain becomes more and more acquainted with following the right educate of concept that doesn't in any way divert from its track. Leaving it unchecked will simplest lead a chain of argumentative essays that can be classified as "monotonous." We aren't looking an animal that desires to be baited into being hunted. There isn't always any want to dawdle inside the returned of a bush. Cajoling your readers within the path of your argument is and need to stay your primary precedence.

2.   Illogical fallacies preserve their cup (as referred to in chapter three) whilst we communicate not unusual errors. In some instances, they may be also embedded in an essay on cause. However, normal cases are because of a loss of hobby and carelessness. Illogical fallacies talk over with manipulating an essay further to the reader into accepting your component of view. Meaning, the

information and proof provided are not extremely good. Leaving the general good judgment for your essay to be puzzled and judged negatively.

A particular example might be advertising and advertising and marketing. Companies use persuasive classified ads to attract greater buyers/clients in shopping for their merchandise. They are one-sided and rely on manipulation more in comparison to keeping information. It is an unimpeachable method over at a advertising and marketing and advertising branch but a violation in argumentative writing.

3. Editing / rechecking is going an extended way. We are regularly capable of refine our sentence shape that, in go back, intensifies the meaning of the sentence with in addition clarity. Minor grammatical errors are inevitable to be determined.

Most importantly, if the hassle of the essay could be very controversial, then rechecking permits to make certain that somewhere alongside the lines, you likely did no longer display lack of knowledge in the direction of a manner of existence, faith, u.S.A. Of the us, and so forth. Any stereotypical reasoning that negates the mind of essential thinking may come into consciousness. Such human errors can disrupt your sincere intentions with out you understanding. We, as humans, have a tendency to be torpid and no longer test toward the give up. By all technique, chorus from you doing so. Surely if you have spent an hour or more writing an essay, you can cope with seven more mins.

four. Set the general tone and diploma of depth wished in accordance with those humans to whom it'll possibly be addressed. A top notch instance might be while doctors give an reason behind a hassle to parents who've now not studied biology and brought clinical publications. Basically, you have to be capable of draw a line among writing for specialists and writing for university students or the overall public. I actually have seen writing styles which could in shape any form of reader as properly. However, such little information are to be more expert. Sometimes the state of affairs additionally asks to provide heed to such information.

After discussing such a number of specifics, Octavia Butler's quote consists of mind.

"You do now not start out writing properly stuff. You start off writing crap and count on it is properly stuff, after which regularly, you get better at it. That's why I say that one of the most precious trends is persistence." A actual essential philosopher will now not continuously be a notable creator. Keep that in thoughts and hold striving for development.

Chapter 14: Significance Of Critical Thinking For Personal Development And The Pursuit Of Wisdom.

This e-book, for the purpose that very begin, has focused its focal factor at the significance of crucial questioning. We, as people, are curious creatures, however curiosity is in no manner ignited indoors parents with out a reason. It continually calls for a supply of obscured expertise simply prepared to be determined or, in this case, an concept.

We are interested in the subjects that deliver forth with them, blessings for our worldly and private income in existence. Critical thinking elevates our private improvement to greater moderen horizons of first-class affirmations. It makes us humble and wiser. As we attain the very climax of this e-book, it's miles crucial to fathom the extents within the path of which crucial wondering contributes to our non-public development. As to the way it well sculptures the satisfactory in us if perfected.

If I take my instance of ways essential questioning has impacted me through the years, then seven attributes come to mind. Researching those very equal attributes made me recognise that they are certainly the most vital ones. If your vital questioning capabilities have helped you got those tendencies, then you are really on the perfect route.

Empathy

Empathy is the functionality of know-how one's feelings and furthermore sharing your non-public. True empathy is best advanced while you discover ways to link exceptional humans's dilemmas for your past or present state of affairs. Helping you to invoke matching emotions as them to in fact paint a picture of what they suggest and are feeling.

In contemporary international, empathy is a huge a part of every art work life in addition to non-public life. In work life, managers and leaders use empathy to evaluate the deeper issues in their personnel. In hopes of putting in a better bond with them and to moreover boom the productiveness diploma inside the place of job, permitting personnel to revel in greater inspired, which, in end result, ends in a higher output charge. In personal lives, empathy is used to enhance socializing. We, people, are social creatures. Empathy allows us make deeply rooted friendships via comprehending our friends thru their personalities and reviews much like the ones we had.

There are three types of empathy. We have cognitive, emotional, and compassionate empathy. Cognitive empathy lets in you to recognize the feelings of people and as to what's making them feel a selected manner. Emotional empathy lets in you to attach emotionally with a person. If a person out of location a years-extended courting, you'll be capable of consolation them by means of the use of telling approximately your failed romance or something identical to their feelings as properly.

Both cognitive and emotional empathy advocates stronger verbal exchange. Lastly, compassionate empathy is the selection for motion. You understood the state of affairs via cognitive empathy and synced emotionally thru emotional empathy. Now, compassionate empathy urges you to useful resource others as a pleasant gesture. For example, a friend of yours does no longer get a challenge for which they had been pretty wonderful that that they had it in the bag. Compassionate empathy will then make you need to take her or him out for dinner, a a laugh night time wherein their mind can be distracted from the disappointment. A little pep communicate in amongst also can growth their morale yet again. Empathy has been of my most impeccable excellent buddy. If it turn out to be not for essential wondering, it's miles almost unreal to assume as to what number of situations would possibly have cause regret because of the absence of empathy.

Invoking A Clearer Lens

A capacity that I consider is a steeply-priced. Critical thinkers are not always excessive achievers in their teachers. I had constantly been a median student whom the academics praised, yet I in no way obtained any form of position among my friends. However, human beings who have always excelled in dominating papers and undertaking high scores regularly do not supply with them, the clean lens to view the sector with. A clearer lens method that you are capable of viewing your environment with sharper observations and know-how.

I typically located myself giving the only of advices to such pals of mine who seem so oblivious of them. They can also moreover have even carried out a difference in examinations; however, their lens to the view worldwide remains fragile and untimely. A clearer lens method having an analytical method with out even knowing it at instances. While others have to clearly stay for every second and kill time, your crystal easy lens that has been invoked from essential wondering can also want to do a whole lot greater for you. You is probably looking at, comparing, reflecting, and noticing everything in a single glide. The changes in tone, emotions, body language, facial expressions, and any external changes gift as well. You will advantage a mentality this is conscious and some distance from any element of surprises along the way, allowing you to analyze each and each detail of existence as you are making your way to more current places; a few would possibly say that this is the initial most skills unlocked from becoming a important truth seeker. Though it is probably proper, it is a capability that by no means stops evolving as well.

Not Being Timorous

Lack of self belief can be the maximum critical obstacle to jump over in life almost about seizing more moderen possibilities for one's non-public sake. However, chapters quantity three and 4 have given conclusive evidence as to how important thinking can make you an intimidating parent within the the front of the opposition in addition to arguments. Critical questioning amplifies verbal exchange via logical and intelligently planned out information and rhetorical speech. Allowing you to stand your floor toward those who've a lesser mind to match yours, it helps you stand on a pedestal loads higher so that you may moreover in no way have to say, "what if?" When your very private heart, thoughts, and soul cajole you in phrases of tactics heaps particular you communicate thru your important thinking, being timorous can be out of doors the massive picture of your hedonism.

DECISIVENESS and EFFECTIVENESS

This gain is a end result of becoming more confident. Being capable enough to make the proper desire out of all given alternatives. If there isn't an opportunity, then it is being sly and intellectually conscious sufficient to create your suitable preference. In exclusive words, it's far the electricity that consists of critical wondering. Not only do you are making well picks, however you are also able to being versatile. Changing your regular rituals if you have to for a new given situation that dreams it. Leading to the simultaneous enhancement of effectiveness as properly, Time is of the essence, and effectiveness allow you to higher plan time manipulate. Good preference making in terms of time desk and getting paintings finished within the best way. Perhaps now, you are beginning to contemplate as to how essential wondering does embody our whole non-public development. From one nook to others, there can be a useful link to which the trait of getting critical questioning is accountable of. As stated earlier than, fear no longer, the hazard of failure. We can't query the elements that make us human. Just like we do now not question as to why we bleed, chances of messing up want to not be harassed upon either. As lengthy as you've got got the studies, the expertise, the statement, and your nicely-made argument, you want to enforce it wholeheartedly.

Helping Those Who Cannot Think For Themselves

Above, I said friends in my life who, irrespective of the truth which can be far brainier as compared to me, do have problem thinking for themselves. They do not own the lens that we vital thinkers have been talented with.

There isn't always any use for this form of understanding if we can not assist people who are unaware of its advantages. The worldwide we stay in is already complete of machinations designed to undermine others in terms of achievement and happiness. Not an inviting vicinity in every corner. Thus, why want to we allow everyone be taken gain of or left within the again of in those consistent mental wars of questioning?

We mentioned empathy, did we not? If we dropped down in reminiscence lane proper now, I am pleasant absolutely everyone have been taken advantage of, cheated and misled due to human beings's lust for worldly pleasures. Therefore it goes with out questioning that we can't label ourselves as vital thinkers if we had been to discard empathy in this depend.

Help with the reason of education as nicely. Wisdom ought to continuously be passed on and not hoarded like it is a few shape of wealth or treasure. Advocate the reason of becoming a lighthouse for those who are out of location of their seas of false impression and thoughts of simplicity; mind which can be too raw and beginner to be taken out inside the real international of practicality.

Eradicator Of Pride And Egoism

The maximum unfavourable trends one have to have to blind themselves of the perks given out from important wondering. While vital wondering revolves throughout the entire universe around us, having delight and an egotistical mindset is self-focused. There may be no non-public development thru being haughty and being ignorant of different people's teachings. Both delight and egoism save you you from breaking out of the shell. At the same time, they manipulate you in wondering in any other case as properly. An phantasm in which in region of a clearer lens, all you spot is an exaggerated self-reflected photograph of your self. A reflect that could praise you and yet is translucent to the relaxation of the arena, Critical thinking demolishes the ones trends and lets in you to view the bigger photograph.

"The one that plants timber, knowing that he is going to never take a seat of their color, has as a minimum commenced to apprehend the this means that of lifestyles." ~ Rabindranath Tagore.

Self-Actualization

The very last piece of the puzzle we label as "private increase." It is not easy. We all were cranky and stubborn. We have hated and saved grudges. Not to mention, we've got minimized our progression in the worldwide we stay in with the resource of not admitting to our flaws. Self-actualization is that art work, wherein matters are first-class intended to be repaired and moved by myself.

Hatchets are buried, errors are ordinary, and advices are professional. Critical questioning itself is a definition of self-tracking and self-reflecting. If you are steadfast for your avenue to turning into essential questioning, then self-actualization is inevitable.

Your dreams of existence remain untouched and undisturbed via self-actualization. They are a motive, and self-actualization keeps that purpose alive and wealthy. Since all of your power is meant to be contributed to those desires and no longer on silly arguments or grudges. One of the maximum thankful components of self-actualization is making someone humbler.

You will no longer be agitated by using manner of worldly pleasures together with wealth, homes, or any other supply of boasting. Hedonism will on my own be the route you may pick out out out to stroll on. Whatever technique that you'll be wanting to make that journey, you may be more than thankful to have had them. The idea of having extra is some trouble you will leave inside the hands of the universe.

Chapter 15: The Theory of Critical Thinking

In this bankruptcy, you will studies the essential additives of important questioning and why it's miles critical to encompass this manner whilst making life picks. It is disconcerting to realise that quite a few us undergo existence on autopilot, making crucial choices that are not primarily based completely mostly on right reasoning. Simply placed, we've got now turn out to be privy to jumping to conclusions approximately the whole thing spherical us.

The outcomes are clean to look. By time and again ignoring what our mind is telling us and relying extra on feelings and assumptions, we are continuously suffering to repair the results of horrible preference making. On pinnacle of that, maximum human beings have turn out to be increasingly more indecisive, in reality because of the truth they not consider of their potential to make the proper choices.

Why do we get hold of to stay like this?

I need to expose you the manner important questioning can end up the bedrock of your selection-making manner. But first, we want to dig deeper into what crucial thinking is and the manner it can benefit you.

What Is Critical Thinking?

Critical thinking can be defined as your capacity to system thoughts in a clear and rational manner. It is your potential to have a observe one-of-a-type thoughts and understand how they'll be all logically connected and correlated. It sounds clean enough. In truth, it is simple to count on that crucial thinking is something we do quite a few every day, proper?

Let me ask you a smooth query. If you study the u . S . A . Of the society round you nowadays, are you able to virtually say that vital questioning is pervasive? Do the majority of the people use reasoning to determine the fact from the faux? If most human beings tried to use critical wondering before you decide, we wouldn't want to deal with one many of the maximum crucial annoying situations in recent times – concerning fake data because the reality, in desire to recognizing it for what it in reality is. In financial disaster twelve, I will show you a manner to region into effect crucial wondering to research faux data.

I need to break down the concept of critical thinking with the aid of the usage of highlighting some of its key additives. If you can observe the ones specific additives, you will be capable of use reasoning to differentiate among truth and lies in regular life. The components of critical thinking encompass:

• Understanding commonplace experience and logical fallacies. Logical fallacies are portions of faux reasoning which humans use to deceive and control others.

• Differentiating amongst information and private opinions.

• Maintaining equity and open-mindedness. You want to now not brush aside or get hold of any piece of records without investigating it first.

• Constantly asking inquiries to discover the truth. Learn to impeach your very very own thoughts similarly to the ones of others.

- Self-regulating your very own belief strategies so you do not get tripped up by means of way of logical fallacies.

To be a essential logician, you need to learn how to be open-minded and pay attention to all factors of view, even in case you do now not agree with them. Tools collectively with not unusual experience, revel in, and studies may be associated with dig up the reality, no matter the reality that it's miles hidden beneath a mountain of lies. This is how a critical logician will become manipulation-evidence, pragmatic and higher able to make a selection.

Becoming a Critical Thinker

To come to be a vital thinker, you need to increase the potential to interact in impartial and reflective questioning. I want to admit that this is some thing that is very hard to do in a global wherein we are continuously bombarded with records from advertisers, political occasions, and friends and own family (through social media). It's like our whole lives were decreased all the manner all the manner right down to anything the following belief leader has to mention. We in the intervening time are familiar with sitting passively and receiving facts in choice to activating our minds and punctiliously wondering the thoughts and ideals which is probably being shoved down our throats.

As a important truth seeker, you should first broaden the talents to evaluate whether or not the arguments that someone or frame is making are a legitimate example of the complete photograph. Then you want to go a step in addition and prepare your self to just accept that perhaps what you believed to be actual, isn't, and vice versa.

For instance, if someone tells you that all cats with blue eyes are evil, and, traditionally, you have got been attacked through a blue-eyed cat as a infant, might no longer it's accurate a terrific manner to take delivery of that announcement? Most human beings should, really because of the truth they might be counting on beyond opinions to make a judgement, with out bothering to move the greater mile by manner of manner of really gaining knowledge of what it manner to be an evil, blue-eyed cat.

Hence critical wondering ought to in no way be primarily based on instinct or emotions. You want to learn how to make selections by using manner of figuring out mistakes in reasoning and assessing your non-public private ideals and assumptions. To do that effectively, you can want to observe a few very specific abilities.

Critical Thinking Skills

To end up a essential philosopher, you have to be familiar with a enormous set of talents which includes declaration, studies, inference, interpretation, reflected image, problem-solving, assessment, rationalization, and desire making.

Those are the overall abilties, however permit me damage them down in addition and highlight the precise abilities you want for vital thinking. You need to learn how to:

• Think approximately an trouble objectively and severely.

- Understand how various mind are inter-connected.

- Identify numerous arguments being made about an hassle.

- Examine a factor of view and test its validity.

- Recognize any weaknesses in an trouble or the evidence supplied.

- Identify the capability implications of a person's argument or announcement.

- Provide installation excellent judgment and basis for every argument you want to make.

All the above talents will are available in handy at the identical time as questioning drastically. However, there may be one key detail which you also want to growth. This is foresight. Foresight is truely thinking systematically approximately functionality destiny activities at the same time as making choices in recent times.

Let's say which you are a company proprietor. You recognize that you may decorate your functionality output if you moved your corporation to some special area. However, it moreover dawns on you that in case you circulate your enterprise to a much off region, your maximum expert personnel received't be capable of circulate with you. What do you do? Do you pick to transport after a larger earnings potential and lose most of your first-rate employees, or do you live located and preserve your expert employees?

You need to look at this problem in a manner a good way to reduce the impact of the war. Critical questioning requires which you make a tentative desire, research it, and then determine how that desire may additionally have an effect on your commercial organisation, employees, and the community spherical you. There may be such a lot of various factors that you have not however considered, and it's miles great with the resource of using the usage of foresight that you may see the capability risks of making any unique surrender.

This is in reality an instance of techniques critical important questioning talents are at the same time as going through real-existence worrying conditions every single day.

Purpose of Critical Thinking

Different people have precise motives for the use of important thinking, depending on their events. However, the precise competencies said above need to be utilized by all people who desires to have a look at vital questioning. Critical wondering have to normally lead you to the great viable solution or end.

To make the high-quality use of vital thinking, you first have to determine what you want to obtain objectively. For example, if you are having a verbal exchange with someone, you need to find out in case your purpose conflicts with theirs. If you are seeking out the awesome dog breed for your home, and that they need you to undertake the stray dog in their outside, then there can be a potential warfare.

But if you check this example considerably, you could additionally recognize that there are a few questions you need to answer. You say you want the outstanding canine breed, but what does the phrase 'top notch' propose to you? What makes any precise breed the fine? Are you searching out a canine that could stay home on my own all day without laid low with separation anxiety? Do you want a breed that loves playing with children? Are you seeking out a watchdog or a partner canine?

As you may see, 'fantastic' doesn't in reality say hundreds, so it obtained't assist you clear up the warfare. But you'll only understand this when you pause to think what 'fantastic' approach for you. Once you have were given have been given clarified exactly what you need from a canine, you'll be surprised to find out that the stray inside the out of doors is the satisfactory breed for you and your own family.

The essential purpose of all vital thinkers is to get to the fact. So lengthy as you have the fact, you'll by no means be afraid of truly anyone who comes at you with an opposing view. You may be decisive at the same time as making choices and there received't be any doubt to keep you back from moving in advance. If you find out that you are incorrect, you may be given your mistake and trade direction.

But attending to the fact can be quite a undertaking. Why do I say this? Most regularly than no longer, what we call 'the reality' is typically tainted by way of the use of way of private beliefs. When making a decision, you might imagine that it is primarily based mostly on the fact, but in truth, it's miles definitely your private likes, dislikes, alternatives, and biases which may be clouding your capacity to count on absolutely. All the ones elements make it hard to make the right choice and may even save you you from making any choice the least bit. You grow to be turning into wishy-washy and unsure of your self.

However, with the useful useful resource of the use of essential thinking, you may start the choice-making way via accepting which you do have biases and alternatives. Then at every degree of the selection-making manner, you will keep in mind how the ones biases are affecting your wondering. In essence, you will have to get a higher idea of who you're in advance than you may pass judgement for your state of affairs.

You want to learn how to adjust your wondering so that you prevent taking a positive stance surely because you're already emotionally related to it. Just because of the truth you assist a favourite crew doesn't propose you shield every motion that its gamers take. Sometimes we even take a advantageous stand really to spite the alternative person within the argument. How frequently have you ever ever supported a desire surely to make a person else look horrible or because of the fact you feel grumpy? These are all factors you need to be aware about even as making picks.

This is the point I need to make here. As lengthy as you stay privy to your strengths and weaknesses whilst making a decision, you may increase the possibilities of getting a effective vital wondering gadget.

Simplified Critical Thinking Exercise

In this section, I'm going to recognition on a clean workout that will let you recognize how the vital wondering technique works. We will bypass deeper into essential wondering strategies in a later economic catastrophe.

From what we've got cited to this point, it is able to seem that critical questioning is a complicated concept that could be a battle to use in normal lifestyles. However, I want to detail out a few difficulty this is essential in allaying such mind.

Nobody on the face of this planet thinks severely one hundred percent of the time. There are times whilst we lose our feel of strength of mind and assume in random and unsystematic techniques. For example, at the same time as we lose a cherished one, we're probably to make alternatives without questioning them through. We can without problem be conquer through grief and anger, and every person recognize how irrational your thoughts can get when conquer with the resource of these feelings.

On the other hand, going via an ecstatic revel in also can make you lose electricity of will.

Just ask any fan of the nowadays-topped 2018 Super Bowl champions, the Philadelphia Eagles. It is mentioned that some enthusiasts climbed on top of balconies, mild poles, and avenue signs and symptoms and jumped into the crowds underneath. Since their institution is known as after a fowl, the ones enthusiasts made the choice to strive out their flying abilties! These were normal human beings making choices that were now not notably belief thru.

The detail I'm trying to make is that vital wondering is a information that you'll use relying for your gift thoughts-set. The brilliant problem to do is learn how to decorate your essential thinking abilties as masses as viable so that after the time comes, you may be equipped to use them to remedy any problem. All you need is exercise and staying power.

Go earlier and attempt the following workout.

Think of a few element that you have been informed nowadays. Now ask yourself those questions:

1.   Who made the assertion? Was it someone you are acquainted with? Was it someone in a role of power or authority? Does it even keep in mind range who said it?

2.   What did the man or woman say? Were they offering records or have turn out to be it an opinion? Did they present all the facts or simply some of the data?

three.   Where did the individual say it? Was the communication in a personal or public vicinity? Were others given an possibility to reply and offer an opportunity mind-set?

4.   When did they make the declaration? Was it prior to, sooner or later of, or after a primary event? Does the timing rely?

five.   Why did the man or woman make the declaration? Did they supply a purpose why they keep that unique opinion? Was their purpose to make a specific character appearance lousy or pinnacle?

6.   How have become it said? Was the individual unhappy, glad, angry, or detached? Was the declaration verbal or written? Were you capable of apprehend what was stated?

Follow those clean steps and inquiries to jumpstart your essential wondering machine.

Chapter Summary

Here are the important thing factors of the financial ruin:

- Critical thinking is the functionality to way thoughts in an analytical and rational way.

- The intention of crucial wondering is to make the superb decision and achieve the high-quality final consequences feasible in every scenario.

- Critical wondering requires a famous set of abilities which includes commentary, research, inference, interpretation, pondered image, trouble-fixing, assessment, clarification, and choice making.

- The reason of all important thinkers is to get to the truth. This reality need to not be clouded via private options, bias and stereotypes.

- To think substantially, you want to be aware of the effect your strengths, weaknesses, and biases must your choice-making method.

- One of the critical element factors of crucial questioning is foresight. You want to look the future effect of your alternatives in advance than making them.

- You can't suppose critically approximately each unmarried scenario. However, you may workout the competencies essential so that you are generally organized to make the outstanding preference feasible.

- Asking the proper questions can often assist you beautify your capability to suppose considerably.

In the following monetary disaster, you could find out about deductive and inductive reasoning.

Chapter 16: Deductive and Inductive Reasoning

In this financial smash, you'll find out about two strategies normally used while sporting out medical research. These methods are Deductive and Inductive reasoning.

So, how are inductive and deductive reasoning relevant to vital thinking and desire making?

If you need to emerge as a important thinker, you need to learn how to query the entirety. Critical thinkers are generally inclined to use something equipment they have got, to find the reality, even though it isn't simply glaring. One of these equipment, as we've got seen in previous chapters, is studies.

When you're carrying out studies, you can come across masses of data, normally in the shape of arguments. An argument is a announcement (or premise) this is made and the corresponding stop this is drawn from it. For instance, "Bingo is a dog. All dogs have 4 legs. Therefore, Bingo has 4 legs." This is a conventional argument that has statements and a end.

However, the hassle with research is that some of the arguments you will encounter may not be actually accurate. Some may be flat out lies. In order to determine whether you are handling a true announcement or a faux one, you want to use deductive and inductive reasoning.

In a nutshell, you can not begin essential questioning or choice making with out first the use of the ones techniques to confirm the authenticity of your information.

Now, permit's dive deeper into deductive and inductive reasoning.

Deductive Reasoning

When using deductive reasoning, you start out with a idea (or speculation) and then look for proof to show whether or now not the concept is genuine. This approach is typically everyday as the identical old for project studies. You begin with a deductive argument and then art work your way deeper till you get a few sturdy truth.

When the use of deductive reasoning to reveal a idea, all you want to do is choose and examine some specific examples or times. If you discover that those few instances are true, then you could very well expect that each one instances internal that famous elegance also are true.

Let's test some easy examples of deductive reasoning:

- All women are mortal. Mary is a lady. Therefore, Mary is mortal.

- If there is smoke, a few detail is burning. There is smoke within the room. Therefore, something is burning inside the room.

From the 2 examples above, we're capable of see that if the primary premises are proper, then the conclusion want to furthermore be real. With deductive reasoning, you should be able to show the conclusions to be real as long as the premises are accurate.

But the query that needs to be spoke back is that this: How will I recognise if the premises that a person is the usage of are actual?

This is in which research is to be had in. If you test the easy examples we have used up to now, it shouldn't be too hard to prove that Bingo is a canine, Mary is mortal or that smoke is a sign of some thing burning. The research here could be through remark.

However, even as faced with the greater complicated arguments that we study inside the media, you need to verify the premises from pretty a few sources and take a look at the credentials of whoever authored the tale. You should no longer blindly take delivery of the sound bytes and biased critiques which have emerge as so not unusual in essential records networks. You surely need to learn how to truth check, no matter how time-eating this could be.

If someone on TV is being interviewed about a bill that is being cited with the useful aid of the Senate, you want to log on to senate.Gov and verify what they will be announcing. If you have the invoice range, input it into the quest box and look at the invoice yourself.

Another way to authenticate the premises of an difficulty is thru relying on your non-public personal revel in. If you stay in a selected community and a person remarks that,

"Everyone in this community loves cats," you want with a purpose to refute this declare from personal revel in. You stay in the community, however you don't love cats. Therefore, that may be a fake argument.

The great hassle you may need to contend whilst the use of personal enjoy in choice to investigate is your personal private bias. Be careful that you do no longer permit your paradigms to cloud your reasoning.

Inductive Reasoning

When using inductive reasoning, you first accumulate all your data, study it, after which growth a idea based on what you've got got have been given observed. This is the alternative method to deductive reasoning, in which case, you begin through the use of looking particular examples of inclinations and events in actual lifestyles and then come to be with a huge generalization or principle based totally on what you've got were given seen.

Unlike a deductive argument, an inductive argument isn't always continuously considered valid. We virtually say that the argument is powerful. This is due to the truth an inductive argument never gives complete beneficial resource to confirm its end.

For example, you could take a look at that if a father is a businessman, then there can be a immoderate hazard that the sons might also grow to be businessmen. Therefore, your quit is that the entrepreneurial pressure is inherited. However, your precept received't be really accurate. There are nonetheless many exclusive theories that may be supported through way of the precise equal information. It is possible that the sons went into commercial organisation because of the behavior and have an effect on of their father, now not their genes.

When using inductive reasoning, the vital detail to endure in mind is that the precept you give you even though offers a logical clarification of the facts you have gathered. It might be illogical to turn the argument round and say that entrepreneurial dad and mom have no effect on the entrepreneurial pressure in their kids. The proof does not assist that hypothesis the least bit.

Here are some examples of inductive reasoning at artwork:

- My cat is white. Your cat is white. His cat is white. Therefore, all cats are white.

- The majority of Siamese cats have blue eyes. Furry is a Siamese cat. Therefore, Furry in all likelihood has blue eyes.

- The majority of universities in Texas ban alcohol on campus. Therefore, the bulk of universities in America ban alcohol on campus.

It is plain to appearance that deductive reasoning is more targeted from the outset and can be used to confirm a concept. Inductive reasoning has an inclination to be greater exploratory within the starting. However, on their very own, neither of those can be used to make a effective argument.

Deduction offers strong proof, however it never is based on any real-worldwide observations or experiments to check its premises. Induction, as a substitute, is based an excessive amount of on announcement however in no manner without a doubt comes near forming a reputable idea. That is why you're higher off the use of each procedures while task your studies.

Deductive and Inductive Fallacies

If you're taking be aware of the records or study the numerous blogs and articles everywhere in the internet, you're likely to encounter a few fallacies. In reality, with the technology of faux information, there are various fallacies to be had. A fallacy is actually a end which you arrive at because of lousy reasoning.

A deductive fallacy is wherein your quit may be right or fake, despite the fact that your premises are correct. For example:

"All monkeys can climb timber. My cat isn't always a monkey. Therefore, my cat cannot climb wooden."

In the example above, you can't say with truth that your cat can't climb trees in reality because he isn't a monkey. At the equal time, it is able to be authentic that your cat can be unable to climb bushes. The premises are actual, but your cease can also want to move both way.

An inductive fallacy is in that you're creating a cease even though your premises are not sturdy enough to guide your element of view. For example:

"Bingo is the simplest German Shepherd I recognize. Bingo is calm and quality. Therefore, German Shepherds are calm and super dogs."

This is referred to as a hasty generalization. You are taking the case of one German Shepherd and assuming that all of them behave inside the identical way as your canine. This is how we become generalizing a whole race, gender, or nationality virtually due to the fact we're too short to make conclusions based on inclined premises.

Chapter Summary

Here are the essential factor elements of the financial ruin:

- To use your important thinking capabilities and make alternatives, you want to depend upon studies. Since studies records may be faulty, you want to apply deductive and inductive reasoning to get to the reality.

- An argument includes a premise and the corresponding end this is drawn from it.

- Deductive reasoning includes starting up with a principle after which seeking out evidence to show whether or now not the concept is actual or faux.

- To authenticate a premise, you have to conduct studies. This may be via observation, literature study, or non-public revel in.

- Inductive reasoning consists of first amassing all your data, reading it, after which growing a idea primarily based totally totally on what you've got decided.

- With inductive reasoning, the premises can be actual, however we're capable of in no manner say that the perception is proper. The maximum we are capable of do is agree that the perception is strong.

- Most researchers use each deductive and inductive reasoning when you keep in mind that none of these techniques may be powerful on their personal.

- In a deductive fallacy, your quit can be actual or fake, regardless of the reality that your premises are correct.

- In an inductive fallacy, you are making a end in spite of the reality that your premises are not strong sufficient to aid your issue of view.

In the following financial disaster, you may analyze a number of the steps which might be applied in crucial thinking.

www.ingramcontent.com/pod-product-compliance
Lightning Source LLC
Chambersburg PA
CBHW062139020426
42335CB00013B/1267